W. Wheeler

Original Poetry

Consisting of Psalms, Hymns and Spiritual Songs

W. Wheeler

Original Poetry
Consisting of Psalms, Hymns and Spiritual Songs

ISBN/EAN: 9783744776554

Printed in Europe, USA, Canada, Australia, Japan

Cover: Foto ©Lupo / pixelio.de

More available books at **www.hansebooks.com**

ORIGINAL POETRY.

CONSISTING OF

PSALMS, HYMNS,

AND

SPIRITUAL SONGS, Etc.

INCLUDING SOME ON THE PROPHECIES,

RELATING TO

THE GRAND MILLENNIUM!

OR

REIGN OF SAINTS UPON THE EARTH!

LONDON:
WERTHEIMER, LEA AND CO., PRINTERS,
FINSBURY CIRCUS.

INTRODUCTORY REMARKS.

It will not be denied, I presume, by persons who are the best informed, and of the most enlightened judgment, that the reading of compositions in verse on scriptural subjects may be both interesting, instructive, and profitable, as the mind of the reader is prepared to understand and receive the vital truths contained in the selected portions of "holy writ." Under such impressions, the greater proportion of the following pieces were penned and published, and which will, I believe, tend to elucidate some of the most striking and remarkable passages found in the "Book of Books."

Nor will it be denied that many of the sections of the Catholic, or universally professing Christian Church, believe singing of psalms and hymns to constitute a very important part of Christian worship; and, therefore, it may be well for us to consider the teaching of the New Testament on this sublime and interesting subject. Here I submit that singing is spoken of more as a personal than as a general associated duty, Ephe. 5, 19. "*Speaking to yourselves* in psalms and hymns and spiritual songs: singing and making melody in your heart to the Lord." Col. iii. 16. "Let the word of Christ dwell in you richly in all wisdom : *teaching and admonishing one another* in psalms and hymns and spiritual songs, singing with grace in your hearts to the Lord."

We are assured by Jesus Christ himself that no worship is acceptable to God unless it be in spirit and in truth, John 4, 23-24; and such worship necessarily implies the exercise of living faith, for whatsoever is not of faith is sin, Rom. 14, 23; hence said the great Apostle Saint Paul, "I will pray with the spirit, and I will pray with the understanding also; I will sing with the spirit, and I will sing with the understanding also," 1 Cor. 14, 15. Here we see a reason why singing is spoken of as a personal and not as a general associated duty, for every Christian knows best when he can utter words in devotional exercises and religious worship under a right feeling and influence. That singing was a personal and not a general observance is plain from the Apostle's testimony of the practice of the Corinthian Christians in their religious assemblies, 1 Cor. 14, 26.

James, also speaks of singing as a personal exercise, Jam. 5, 13. Some of the compositions referred to in this book as psalms, hymns, and spiritual songs, will be found suitable for devotional purposes, and may be used by believers as such in their *Christian liberty*, or they may be read, as the mind of each is spiritually disposed, for the elucidation of scriptural truth and the acquisition of religious knowledge.

I have (as a rule) given the measures of each separate composition, which may help to furnish a ready assistance to the general reader.

The pieces are arranged as far as practicable in Biblical order, so that any selected piece may be more easily found.

If any good should result from this effort to discharge a Christian duty and obligation, as all good is from God, my desire is that He may have the praise.

W. W.

THAME, 1874.

PROLOGUE IN ACROSTICS.

P raise waiteth for the Lord above,
S ion the Church waiteth the same,
A nd soon the spirit of grace will move
L oud hallelujahs to His name :
M oving in earth and heav'n above,
S ongs of the purest praise and love.

H is church in mourning will appear,
Y earning her bridegroom's voice to hear,
M aintain His truth with one accord,
N arrating too His promised word,
S ighing and fainting for her Lord.

A nd soon the seventh trump will sound,
N ations and peoples to confound,
D isclosing terrors all around.

S torms of dread wrath will then begin,
P unished the world will be for sin,
I rreligion be clearly shown,
R epresented and fully known,
I n its every dress be seen,
T ested as it never had been,
U nder every form and mien,
A nd be exposed to ev'ry eye,
L anguishing in its misery.

S ongs to the righteous follow, and
O n all the earth in ev'ry land,
N ear or far off they are as one,
G overned by Christ, the *mystic stone*,
S erving the Lord, and Him alone !

E vents of providential birth,
T o produce changes on the earth :
C onclude with times of golden worth !

PSALMS, HYMNS, SPIRITUAL SONGS,

ETC.

CREATION. L. M.

Gen. i. 1—5.

1. In the beginning God hath said
Both the heavens and earth were made.
He speaks in language most sublime,
Also, in reference to time—

For time alone beginning has,
Before time no beginning was!
And time alone we may depend
Hath a beginning and an end.

As darkness covered all the deep,
The earth, one vast and confused heap,
Was without form, empty and void,
As if by rebel pow'rs destroyed.

To chaos, brooded o'er with night,
God spake and said, "Let there be light!" *
Then light did into being spring,
And sped abroad with fleetest wing.

The heav'n and earth of which we read,
Of them th' Spirit of God hath said,
That in six days they finish'd stood,
And were by Him attested good!

* 2 Cor. iv. 6.

Yea, in six days of time alone,
The great Creator's works were done,
And on the *seventh* God did rest—*
The day He sanctified and blest.

CREATION. C. M.

Gen. i. 14—19.

2. God created the sun and moon,
    And all the stars of heav'n,
Which shone out brightly very soon,
    As they for lights were giv'n.

And signs and seasons, days and years,
    As time should onward move,
Such were their uses, it appears,
    And such they always prove.

The sun doth light and heat impart
    To all things here below,
Just like a centre or a heart
    From which their life must flow.

The moon and stars they yield their light,
    And constant service give
To such as move on earth by night,
    Or on the ocean drive.

Their outward uses various are,
    And he that learns them well,
He in their benefits may share,
    And such to others tell.

They also greater lessons give,
    And he that so inclines
Their higher teaching to receive,
    May read in them the *signs !*

* Gen. ii. 2, 3.

CREATION.

C. M.

Gen. i. 20—25.

3. God, He created ev'ry beast
  Which on the earth may rove,
 Both from the greatest to the least,
  Yea, all that live and move.

 He made the lion without fear,
  Wherever he may roam;
 The howling wolf and savage bear,
  Which seek a forest home.

 And ev'ry character we find,
  With ev'ry form pourtray'd,
 In beasts and birds of ev'ry kind,
  Which God in wisdom made.

 He made the monsters of the deep,
  And the strange creatures there;
 With all that swim and all that creep
  In waters ev'rywhere.

 He made the trees and ev'ry plant,*
  And ev'ry flower that blows,
 With all green grass and herbs extant,
  And ev'ry thing that grows.

 And all things that are seen or known
  Unto the human race,
 Are by unerring wisdom shown
  To have their use or place.

 So ev'ry thing on earth is good,
  If known and used aright;
 For physic, clothing, or for food,
  For comfort or delight.

* i. 11, 12.

CREATION.

S. M.

Man made in the image and likeness of God.
Gen. 26—27.

4. Man in God's image made,
   Was with rich graces stor'd;
   His rule on earth all things obey'd,
   And own'd him as their lord.

   He was their proper head,
   Appointed so by God.
   The creatures owed him a just dread,
   And full subjection show'd.

   He gave each one its name,*
   And ev'ry name exprest
   The qualities from which it came,
   And character imprest!

   His knowledge it was great,
   His understanding sure;
   In him true wisdom had her seat,
   And all his works were pure.

   Thus he in righteousness
   And holiness divine,
   God's living *image* did express
   And in his *likeness* shine!

   His Hierarch in place,
   Obedient to His Word;
   A Son of God by special grace,
   An angel of the Lord.

PRAISE FOR THE CREATION.

L. M.

Gen. ii. 1.

5. Awake, my soul, and sound His praise,
   Who did the world's vast fabric raise;
   Th' Almighty Word who spake at first,†
   When all from gloomy chaos burst.

* ii 19, 20.   † John i. 1—3   Psa. xxxiii. 6.

Order out of disorder sprang,
While the admiring Angels sang ;*
Yea, hosts whose praise the heav'ns employ,
Arose and shouted for the joy.

Where'er I turn my eyes below,
What wisdom doth creation show :
Who can descry the secrets there,
Or all His wondrous works declare ?

Or if above I lift my eyes,
And view the glories of the skies,
I sink in silence, and adore
The God who lives for evermore.

ADAM'S PROBATION AND FALL.

Gen. ii. 7—9, 15—25 ; and iii. 1—19.

6. When Adam in Paradise stood,
    The garden of Eden to keep,
Surrounded with every good,
    He neither knew hunger nor sleep.

He, in his creation, was pure,
    And had his well-being in God ;
But did not his *trial* endure,
    For Nature his spirit had woo'd.

Then Adam grew weary, and slept
    On th' earth which his love had endear'd :
Of his virgin state was bereft,†
    And a woman, to help him, appear'd.

The Serpent, most subtle and wise,
    Saw the unsuspecting and fair :
His arts with all diligence plies,
    To ruin this now happy pair.

* Job xxxviii. 7.   † Rev. xiv. 4.

He tempts them to eat of the tree
  Which God did so plainly forbid;
For then, as th' *Gods* they should be,
  But th' sin and its punishment hid.

They ate of its fruit, and they fell,
  Were driven from their happy home:
When th' tale of Redemption must tell
  Of Christ, the *Restorer*, to come!

ADAM AND EVE NO LONGER IN PARADISE. 8's

Gen. iii. 1—19.

7. While in Eden our parents remained,
  How contented and happy they look:
By th' fruits of the garden sustained,
  With water from river or brook.

But soon they from Eden were driv'n,
  For eating of one only tree,
Which th' knowledge of *evil* had giv'n,
  And made them their nakedness see.

They then seek the fruits of the field,
  Eat bread in the sweat of their brow,
Which th' ground to their labor would yield,
  Where thorns and the thistles will grow.

They both good and evil would know
  In every thing they partook:
But in all their changes below,
  Still drank of the river or brook.

The evil which fell in their way
  With all earth's affliction and strife,
They found quite enough in their day,
  Nor would add to the burdens of life.

The knowledge our parents possest,
  And the laws they then would observe,
Would lead them to act for the best,
  And thus their own interest serve.

THE OFFERINGS OF CAIN AND ABEL. L. M.

Gen. iv. 3—7.

8. When Abel offer'd sacrifice,
It did with pure acceptance rise,
As it express'd, with penitence,
A humble faith and confidence.

But Cain his offering prepar'd,
And with a selfish, vain regard:
Not for offences to atone,
But favor sought for service done.

It was the faith that Abel had
In the *first promise* God had made,
That his acceptance did secure,
And made the promis'd mercy sure!

No works of our own righteousness,
Nor fancied goodness we possess,
Without the faith which God inspires,
Will do for service He requires.

As Abel, we should so prepare
Our offerings of praise nd prayer,
That, by His mercy, ever free,
Our off'rings may accepted be.

If we, as sinners, feel our need
Of mercy, through the woman's seed,
Our service will acceptance find
Through Him—the Saviour of mankind.

ENOCH'S TRANSLATION! L. M

Gen. v. 21—24; Heb. xi. 5.

9. Enoch most truly served the Lord;
   He walk'd with God three hundred years,
As inspiration doth record,
   Which faithful testimony bears.

God testified unto him then
    That He his service did approve;
Who walked uprightly before men,
    And wrought the works of faith and love.

The witness of his conscience gave
    Assurance to his pious mind
That God would pure devotion have,
    And his did thus acceptance find.

For suddenly he was not seen—
    The Spirit hath this witness giv'n—
The prophet had translated been,
    And pass'd away from earth to heav'n.

It was through faith, we understand,
    When in an ecstacy of thought,
And by the Lord the Saviour's hand,
    That he was up to glory caught!

Thus he no more on earth is found,
    If sought he must be sought in vain;
He lives where purer joys abound,
    And will eternally remain.

THE DELUGE.   L. M.
Gen. vii.

10. When the old world was lost and drown'd,
    Deluged by universal flood,
The waters more and more abound,
    Till they above the mountains stood.

Those in the Ark were then secure,
    Both man and beast and creeping thing;
Of all that lived on earth before,
    With birds and fowls of ev'ry wing.

Yea, all that in the Ark were found
    During those awful storms of rain,
Were safely borne above the ground
    Until the earth was dry again.

Then the great fountains of the deep
    Were by fierce *earthquakes* torn and rent!
The thunder-clouds they howl and weep,
    Until their storms of wrath are spent!

Torrents of rain are pouring down
    Amidst the forkèd lightning's glare,
Until the earth is overflown,
    And all in the destruction share;

Save such as in the waters dwelt:
    These in their element alive,
The terror and commotion felt,
    Yet the catastrophe survive.

The world once more will be destroy'd,
    And ev'ry earthly life expire;
The wrathful agents then employ'd,
    Will purge with a devouring fire.*

THE APPOINTED TIMES AND SEASONS. L. M.
Gen. viii. 22.

11. He who the universe sustains,
    Said, while the earth for man remains,
    Summer and winter shall not cease,
    Nor heat and cold in their degrees.

    There always should be day and night,
    Hours of darkness and hours of light;
    Seed time and harvest to befriend,
    Till man's terrestrial state shall end.

    These foretold truths which God supplied,
    Hundreds of years have ratified;
    And hundreds more may yet remain
    To ratify their truth again.

* 2 Pet. iii. 6, 7.

As He from perfect knowledge spake,
Time will its demonstrations make
That what He said remaineth sure
Until this world shall be no more.

THE RAINBOW OF PROMISE!   S's
Gen. ix. 12—17.

12. By th' beautiful bow in the cloud,
    Reflected in sunshine and rain,
God speaketh His promise aloud,
    And maketh His covenant plain.

That th' waters which deluged the earth,
    When th' deeps of the ocean were riven,
And th' Almighty's *fiat* went forth
    To open th' floodgates of heaven!

When all earthly lives were destroyed,
    The world and its creatures were drown'd
That th' elements then so employed
    Should never again so abound.

And oft in the sunshine and rain
    The covenant's token is given,
And th' promise repeated again,
    When His bow is seen in the heaven!

NIMROD, THE MIGHTY HUNTER, BEFORE THE LORD!
Gen. x. 8—10.   C. M.

13. Nimrod, the Ruler, fam'd of old,
    A great despotic lord,
Was in exploits of mischief bold,
    And for such acts abhorr'd;

A mighty *hunter* he was found,*
   A spoiler of the good,
Did in oppressive acts abound,
   And stain'd the earth with blood.

A persecutor of all those
   Who bow'd not to his name—
Who would not his religion choose,
   Nor recognise the same.

His kingdom was of great renown,
   And growing more and more,
Exceeded ev'ry other known
   Before his days of yore.

The first great city and its tower,
   Where ancient Babel stood,
Was the beginning of his power,
   To persecute the good!

The city of *confusion* then,†
   Where *Babel* had its birth,
Was th' city of this Nimrod, when
   He reigned upon the earth.

ABRAHAM'S FAITH SHOWN BY HIS OBEDIENCE.

Gen. xii. 1--5.   C. M.

14. Abraham left his father's home:
   He went at God's command,
Expecting better things to come,
   Shadow'd by Canaan's land.

He sojourn'd as a stranger there,
   Yet rich and great became;
Honor'd and rev'renced ev'rywhere,
   A prince of mighty name.

Jer. xvi. 16.   † Gen. x 1—9.

Jehovah did His servant bless,
   Who knew and own'd his pow'r,
In various ways, and numberless
   Did favors on him show'r.

For Abraham believ'd in God,
   As present ev'rywhere;
His faith by his obedience show'd,
   And prov'd his faith sincere.

If we our faith, like him, will show,
   And testimony give
That we th' God of Abraham know,
   And only to Him live,

His providence will us attend,
   And constantly engage
To guide and guard, and us befriend
   Through all our pilgrimage.

GOD THE EXCEEDING GREAT REWARD OF HIS PEOPLE.

Gen. xv. 1.   's.

15. My great and exceeding reward,
   From thee may I never depart;
May Thy Spirit preserve me, and guard
   The issues of life in my heart.

I heard of Thy love with my ears,
   Yet knew not its spiritual worth;
But now it so largely appears,
   That language cannot sound it forth.

In vain is the instrument strung,
   To compass the immortal sound;
It as well on th' willows were hung,
   In the vision of darkness profound.

Yet when, in my weakness, I bear
   A part in the praise of His name,
If a glimpse of His love should appear,
   It raises my soul to a flame.

I feel the sweet impulse of grace,
  Inciting to heavenly mirth;
Enlarged by the light of His face,
  The brightest display of His worth.

No beauty with His may compare,
  In th' mansions of glory above;
His charms the most transporting are,
  In the holiest lustre of love

THE DESTRUCTION OF SODOM AND GOMORRAH.
Gen. xix. 24—25.   L. M.

16. When Sodom and Gomorrah sinn'd,
It harden'd first, then made them blind;
Who were in evil courses driv'n,
Until destroyed from under heav'n.

Prosperity did them surround,*
And pride and idleness abound;
There Satan must have found a seat,
For wickedness had waxen great.†

Their crying sins fierce wrath awakes,
And judgment suddenly o'ertakes;
'Gainst them the elements conspire,
And rain on them brimstone and fire.

God shows by this example giv'n,
Of a strange punishment from heav'n,
When men in wickedness have grown,
Vengeance may smite the sinners down.

ABRAHAM OFFERING UP ISAAC HIS SON!
Gen. xxii. 1—18.   L. M.

17. Abraham went at God's command
  His "only" son to sacrifice;
Followed the leadings of His hand,
  Whose high command would him suffice.

* Eze. xvi. 49, 50.   † Gen. xiii. 13, and xviii. 20, and xix. 13.

He came unto the chosen mount—
    Was it the same where Christ was slain?
If we could not for this account,
    Yet still the *figure* speaketh plain!

He built his altar, framed the wood,
    Bound Isaac, and laid him thereon:
Was then prepared to shed his blood,
    And took the knife to slay his son!

The Angel of the Lord then spake,
    As he had such obedience giv'n:
He would him bless, and also make
    His offspring as the stars of heav'n.

In blessing He would greatly bless,
    And in his promised chosen seed
Every nation should confess
    That God hath blessèd them, indeed.

ABRAHAM'S FAITH DEMONSTRATED BY HIS UNFLINCHING OBEDIENCE. L. M.

Gen. xxii. 1—18; Jas. ii. 21—23.

18. Abraham was the friend of God,
    Who humbly in His service trod;
    Whose faith did him to action move,
    And proved itself by works of love!

Outward profession won't suffice
Without a willing sacrifice.
If God for such an off'ring call,
We should be willing with our all.

Did Abraham refuse to part
With the dear object of his heart
His earthly hopes were fix'd upon,
His promis'd heir, his favor'd son!

So strong was Abraham in faith,
He yielded Isaac unto death.
Thus Isaac, on the altar slain,
Through Abr'ham's faith must live again!

The act approach'd would make him sad,
The act accomplished make him glad;
For God His servant did befriend,
And timely help and succor send.

Thus Abraham obeyed the Lord,
Who spake and promis'd by His Word,
He would him bless in very deed,
And greatly multiply his seed.

What God hath spoken must prevail;
His promises can never fail.
Of this assurances are given
By witnesses in earth and heav'n.

THE WONDERS WROUGHT BY OR THROUGH FAITH IN GOD! L. M.

Exod. iv. 11—17; vii. 1.

19. What mighty wonders have been done
Through living acts of faith alone,
Which human skill nor human power
Could ne'er accomplish nor secure.

Moses, through faith, appears a god,
Commanding changes by his rod.
With it he smote th' Egyptian flood,
And turned its waters into blood.

He holds it forth and frogs appear:
Anon they die and taint the air.
He smote the dust with outstretched arms,
And lice and flies are seen in swarms.

With murrain now their cattle die,
And boils with blains men terrify;
Dread thunders, hail and fire assail,
And all their landed prospects fail.

In clouds devouring locusts come,
And ev'ry green thing left consume;
Thick darkness reigns over the land,
And the *fell* horror none withstand.

Of pestilence he prophesies,
The flower and strength of Egypt dies.
At midnight doth the slaughter spread,
And ev'ry house bemoaned its dead.

He holds his rod towards the sea,
Those mighty waters backward flee.
There Israel journeyed on dry ground,
While the Egyptian host was drown'd.

With Israel in after years,
How wonderful his power appears;
While they by trials were prepar'd
For rest in Canaan, their reward.

A tree made bitter waters sweet,
And flocks of quails arrive for meat;
The manna daily falls for bread,
And water from the rock is shed.

Of lust the murmurers complain,
And thousands are on thousands slain;
Again the ground asunder cleaves,
And the rebellious meet their graves.

The pestilence great numbers slew,
And fiery serpents on them flew:
By their dread bite much people died,
Till faith a remedy applied.

By divers means, in divers ways,
Through faith almighty pow'r displays,
Until the rebels were destroyed,
And all the faithful rest enjoyed.

THE PASCHAL LAMB.   S. M.

Exod. xii. 3—13.

20. The sacred paschal lamb,
    The ancient Jews would slay
That they might sacrifice the same—
    A *figure*, in their day,

    Of Him that was to come—
    Jesus, the Lamb of God!
He, who a body did assume,
    And made it His abode.

    For three-and-thirty years
    After His human birth,
He sojourned in this vale of tears,
    And dwelt as man on earth.

    He well fulfill'd the law,
    And He ended the same;
And those His grace and glory saw *
    Who believed in His name.

    Lo! on the cross He dies;
    There the true Lamb was slain,
A universal sacrifice
    For sins and sinful men!

    The soul of ev'ry type,
    He life and substance gave;
Of all the types the Anti-type,
    And who alone can save.

THE TYPE AND ANTITYPE!   C. M.

Exod. xvii. 6; Numb. xx. 11; 1 Cor. x. 4; Psa. lxxviii. 15, 16.

21. When Moses smote the rock of old,
    The waters issued out
In streams, which Jacob did behold,
    As from a water-spout.

* John i. 14.

This rock, which follow'd Israel
   When in the wilderness,
And did fresh streams with water fill
   To people numberless—

This rock was Christ—their living Lord—
   The just and holy One,
From whom the living waters pour'd,
   In ages past and gone.

This Rock was smitten once for all,
   And all that will receive,
Of Him and drink, for ever shall
   Most freely drink, and live!

The earthly rock was a clear type,
   Where Israel quench'd their thirst,
Of Christ, th' immortal antitype,
   For so that rock was Christ!

From Him the living waters roll,
   In streams for ever pure,
Supplying ev'ry living soul,
   Both now and evermore.

THE TYPE AND ANTITYPE!   L. M.

Exod. xvii. 6; Numb. xx. 11; 1 Cor. x. 4; Psa. lxxviii. 15, 16.

22. Moses, the rock in Horeb smote,
   And gave the people water there!
Then of the miracle he wrote,
   And sent the tidings ev'rywhere.

When he before the people stood,
   And with his rod had struck the rock,
It pour'd forth waters like a flood,
   As if dissevered by the shock.

The water from the mount descends,
 And through the desert streams along :
Israel in its course befriends,
 Serving the wants of old and young.

By Moses' wonder-working rod,
 Both man and beast their thirst allayed ;
The miracle was wrought by God,
 Whom Moses, in the act, obeyed.

Those waters followed Israel,
 By Moses in their journeys led,
And did their Living Rock reveal,
 Who does the living water shed.

The rock pointed to Jesus Christ,
 Who hears His ev'ry creature's call,
And from His glory in the high'st,
 Gives living water unto all.

AMALEK DEFEATED IN BATTLE BY ISRAEL, A JUST PUNISHMENT FOR HIS CRUELTY. L. M.

Exod. xvii. 8—13 ; Deut. xxv. 17—19.

23. Amalek, the foe of Israel,
 Betrayed a base and brutal mind,
When he upon the weary fell,
 And smote the feeble ones behind.

He hesitated not to fight
 Against the people of the Lord ;
And of his pow'r and warlike might
 Hist'ry doth evidence afford.*

Then Joshua, with th' men of war,
 Went out and fought with Amalek ;
While Moses, on the hill afar,
 Did, with his rod, the issue speak.

* Numb. xxiv. 20.

When Moses upwards held his rod,
  Th' Amalekites were beaten down ;
And Israel plainly saw that God
  Alone could them with vict'ry crown.

As when, through weakness, Moses failed,
  His warriors were in evil case :
For Amalek at once prevailed,
  And Israel fled before his face,

By others Moses' hands upheld,
  They turn'd the battle for the day;
The foe was smitten on the field,
  And Israel took the spoils away.

MOSES' ROD POINTING TO HEAVEN SECURED THE VICTORY TO ISRAEL OVER THEIR ENEMIES.

Exod. xvii. 8—13.   8's.

24. When Amalek went out and fought
  With Israel, the people of God,
He from Egypt's bondage had brought,
  Where His signs and wonders He show'd ;

Not alone with their swords and spears,
  Nor with aught they to battle would go,
But through Moses' faith and his pray'rs
  They defeated and conquer'd th' foe,

Pharaoh's host had been overthrown,
  Its terror existed no more ;
Their dead bodies now lay all strewn,
  With their weapons of war on th' shore !

Those weapons did Israel serve
  In their after wars of renown ;
But God did His people preserve,
  And their battles with vict'ry crown.

For when Moses held up his hands,
  As he grasp'd the mystical rod,
Then Israel's victorious bands
  Would see their success was of God!

But when in this duty he failed,
  The same as in pleading for grace,
Then Amalek quickly prevailed,
  And Israel fled from his face.

His arms were then stayèd upright,
  And no more through weakness hang down:
Then Israel waxed valiant in fight,
  And Amalek was overthrown!

THE TEN COMMANDMENTS. L. M.

Exod. xx. 1—17.

25. Jehovah on Mount Sinai spake,
    Before Me ye shall no Gods make;
    No *image* worship shall ye know,
    Of things above or things below.

    Let reason all your acts sustain,
    Nor take the name of God in vain;
    For He will punish such abuse,
    If thoughtlessly His name you use.

    The Sabbath day remember too,
    In it no work or labor do;
    But let it be your highest aim
    To serve the Lord and live to Him.

    Your parents honor and esteem,
    And be obedient unto them.
    Let wisdom guide you from your birth,
    That you may live long on the earth!

No sin to kill shalt thou commit,
For God will surely avenge it;
Man's life must ever sacred be,
In ev'ry tribe and family.

In all things be to others true,
And render unto all their due;
Yea, ev'ry act as sinful deem,
Which you in others would condemn.

Such precepts by the Lord were giv'n,
Who made all things in earth and heav'n;
Who will His blessing also give
To all who shall uprightly live.

SALVATION BY JESUS CHRIST FORESHADOWED BY THE JEWISH PASSOVER. L. M.

Numb. ix. 2—5; John i. 29.

26. When at their sacred feast the Jews
  The lamb in sacrifice had slain,
And when each year the scene renews,
  And the same things were done again:

The lamb was for the supper served,
  And eaten whole with bitter things,*
While other duties were observed,
  And each with it some lesson brings.

But soon those yearly off'rings ceased,
  When Christ a body did assume,
And all were from those rites released,
  When the great anti-type had come!

Hence, at the passover we see
  The slaughtered lamb a *figure* stood,
Of Jesus dying on the tree,
  And shedding there His precious blood!

* Exod. xii. 46; Numb. ix. 12; John xix. 36.

'Twas there the Lamb of God was slain,
   His sacrificial work was done,
And needeth not be done again
   For sin and sinners to atone.

For as by the offence of one
   Judgment and condemnation came,
So by His righteousness alone
   A free salvation through His name.*

ISRAEL'S WELL!   S. M.

Numb. xxi. 16—18.

27. Spring up, O earthly well,
   With flowing waters free,
That we may of its wonders tell,
   When we abundance see.

Thus Israel sang of old,
   When in a desert land,
They did the work of God behold,
   And His work understand.

The princes dug the well,
   Laboring with their staves,
Until the rising waters swell
   In heaving flowing waves.

Water they all desire,
   And water is supplied
For ev'ry service they require,
   And they are satisfied.

* Rom. v. 18.

THE ANTITYPE, OR GOD'S WELL! 8's.

Numb. xxi. 16—18.

28. This well was a type of God's well,
    In spiritual blessings most rife,
  When by His command it doth swell,
    Heave, and flow with the water of life.

  Then all the Lord's people may drink,
    And speak of the waters with joy,
  As they of His goodness will think,
    And their all in His service employ.

  They will sing of th' well of their God,
    As they for its services call:
  When its waters rise up like a flood,
    Supplying the wants of them all.

  Ten thousand times ten thousand may,
    And thousands of thousands around,
  Their thirst with its waters allay,
    Yet, still they flow on and abound!

  They all the Lord's hosts have supplied,
    The armies of Heaven above,
  Who drink to their fill satisfied,
    Or bask in this sea of His love.

"UNTO HIM YE SHALL LISTEN!"

Deut. xviii. 15. 7's. & 6's.

29. Hark, my soul, thy Saviour speaks,
      And inly speaks to thee;
    He thy ev'ry fetter breaks,
      And sets thee wholly free.

    He will scatter all thy chains,
      Till all their weight is gone;
    Slay whate'er of sin remains,
      And rule thy peace alone.

He thy great reward is made,
　　Who once sustain'd the cross;
Glorious hope that cannot fade—
　　That cannot suffer loss.
All that height of bliss is thine,
　　Better than earthly things;
In those palaces divine,
　　Where reigns the King of kings.

GOD FURNISHING THE TABLE OF HIS PEOPLE WITH CHOICE TEMPORAL BLESSINGS.

Deut. xxxii. 13, 14.　　4-6's. & 2-8's.

30.　The table of the Lord
　　　Is with abundance stor'd,
　Which He unto His people grants;
　　　The garden and the field,
　　　From time to time will yield
　A full supply for all their wants.

　　　From earth, from flint and rock
　　　He giveth them a stock
　Of oil and honey for their need;
　　　With butter of the kine,
　　　And milk most rich and fine,
　He doth His chosen people feed.

　　　The best of all the sheep,
　　　From the rich pastures keep,
　And lambs and goats out of the fields,
　　　And finest of the wheat,
　　　He giveth them to eat,
　With all the stores the Ocean yields.

　　　He sent His noble vine,
　　　To furnish them with wine,
　Or pluck the golden fruit as food!*
　　　That if they should be sad,
　　　To cheer and make them glad,
　And praise the Giver of all good.

　　　　　* Micah vii. 1.

CHOICE TEMPORAL BLESSINGS GIVEN BY GOD TO HIS PEOPLE. 8's.

Deut. xxxii. 13, 14.

31. The God of the heavens is nigh
    To all in His name who go forth;
He raiseth His people on high,
    And giveth them blessings on earth.

The stores of the honey and oil,
    The choicest of butter and wheat,
With all the fresh fruits of the soil,
    He giveth His chosen to eat.

The fattest and best of the sheep,
    The lambs and the goats of the flock,
With all the supplies of the deep,
    Which furnish a plentiful stock.

His table of mercies impart
    A freshness and vigor of frame;
His vintage, it cheereth the heart:
    He giveth them wine of the same!

His wisdom and knowledge will teach
    Th' *abuses* and *uses* of food:
The portion that's needful to each,
    Wherein all provision is good.

T' Jeshurun the upright, by God
    The earth's greatest blessings are giv'n;
And t'all in His paths who have trod,
    He will furnish th' highest in heav'n.

JERICHO TAKEN! 8's.

Josh. vi. 1—25.

32. Old Jericho, once walled around,
    Was closely shut up and secured;
When those who within it were found,
    Seemed of its possession assured.

Yet the army of God moved on,
  To compass the city around,
Which in solemn *silence* was done,
  While priests with their trumpets gave sound.

Six days they once all round it go,
  Sev'n times they then compass about,
When trumpets the signal now blow,
  And th' people shout with a great shout:

The wall round the city then fell,
  When they could perform their desire;
They smote all that in it did dwell,
  And burned up the city with fire.

This city may represent men,
  United in their fallen state:
Which like a strong city are seen,
  Well fortified even the gate.

Thus the strong man armed is secure,
  He keepeth his goods there in peace:
Its safety to him would be sure,
  Till a stronger than he take th' place.

So at our great Captain's command,
  We compass the city around;
In *silence* move forward or stand,
  Guided by the trumpet's true sound.

In God's time the wall will fall down,
  His servants ascending straight on,
All before them will be overthrown,
  And the city destroyed when won.

JERICHO'S CURSE AND RESTORATION!   8's.

Josh. vi. 26; 1 Kings xvi. 34; 2 Kings ii. 19—22.

33. Jericho, rebuilt where it stood,
    Was pleasant, as some did declare;
  But its sources of water and food,
    Were sought for and gotten elsewhere.

Its waters some qualities had,
   Which nauseous were to the taste ;
The land, too, was equally bad,
   And hence lay neglected and waste,
'Till Elisha a miracle wrought,
   By the salt put in a new cruse :
To th' spring of the waters he brought,
   On which they their bitterness lose.
The land, too, which drank of the same,
   Although before barren was found,
It now very fruitful became,
   And plenty was seen on the ground.
This representation of force,
   Points at those, while secure in their sin,
Partaking its judgment and curse,
   This city have built up again.
At th' time when such building is raised,
   The work would hang heavy in hand :
Yet th' owners may with it be pleased,
   While barrenness reigns in the land.
And this will continue their case,
   Till they true repentance have sought,
And, enlighten'd by heav'nly grace,
   They are by the true Prophet taught.
Thus th' vessel prepared by the Lord,
   And filled with His all-changing grace,
By this they at last are restor'd,
   And fruitfulness then will take place.

"SO THE SUN STOOD STILL IN THE MIDST OF HEAVEN, AND HASTED NOT TO GO DOWN ABOUT A WHOLE DAY." L. M.

Josh. x. 13.

34. Who will deny that th' sun stood still,
   By Joshua's command, of yore ?
Or that its rotary motion will
   Prove it had not so moved before ?

For God, who made the universe,
　　And did the worlds with light array,
Arrested Nature in her course,
　　About the space of one whole day!

No day like that was ever known
　　Since Adam first in Eden stood;
Or sun with light and heat hath shone,
　　Re-filling all the earth with good.

For God, the all-creating Word,*
　　Who has all things He made upheld,
Did once to man this *sign* afford,
　　And His omnipotence reveal'd!

THE MAN WHO HAD A WELL OF HIS OWN.

2 Sam. xvii. 18.   S. M.

35. The man who had a well,
　　　In his own court or yard,
　He of its benefits could tell,
　　　In which he amply shared.

　　　Inherited by right,
　　　Or with his money bought,
　It would afford him true delight,
　　　If such a good he sought.

　　Where but few wells were known,
　　　And water rarely found,
　A man to have one of his own,
　　　Would make him friends around.

　　　For he that hath a friend,
　　　Must himself friendly show;
　And if he others did befriend,
　　　He would their friendship know.

* John i. 1, 3.

Like bread on waters cast,*
A portion unto seven,
Its own reward may come at last,
And prove a blessing given.

DAVID LONGING FOR WATER OF THE WELL OF BETHLEHEM, AND ITS LESSON? c. m.

2 Sam. xxiii. 13—17; 1 Chron. xi. 15—19.

36. The far-fam'd well of Bethlehem,
As hist'ry doth relate—
The well memorialised by name,
Was near its entrance-gate.

The Philistines, it then appear'd,
Had invaded the land;
King David for this water cared,
And it was near at hand.

With fervent longings does he think,
And utter, as by spell—
"Oh that some one would give me drink,
Out of Bethlehem's well!"

Three mighty heroes, at the cost
Or risk of life and limb,
Brake through the whole Philistines' host,
And brought it unto him!

But David, who, in eager haste,
Had long'd his thirst to quell,
This water would not drink nor taste,
Out of Bethlehem's well.

He pour'd it out before the Lord,
It did so plainly tell
Of lives surrender'd, and restored,
In seeking Bethlehem's well!

* Eccles. xi. 1, 2.

THE MOST HIGH GOD IN HIS ETERNITY!

1 Kings viii. 27; Isa. lvii. 15.   S. M.

37. Jehovah, He is God,
   The high and lofty One;
 O'er worlds unknown extends His rod,
   He ruleth all alone.

   Let angels bow the knee,
   And mortals homage pay;
 The Monarch of eternity
   Bears universal sway.

   Great in His holiness,*
   And fearful in His praise;
 And wonders wrought in righteousness,
   His matchless honors raise.

   From His exalted place,
   That's far above the skies,
 He rules His people by His grace,
   And awes His enemies.

   The terrors of His frown,†
   Rebellious men will slay;
 His arm will beat their madness down,
   And fill them with dismay.

   Let sinners learn to fear,
   Lest by His wrath prepar'd,
 He smite and no deliv'rer near,
   T' avert the just award.

ELIJAH'S RETREAT!

1 Kings xvii. and xviii.   S's.

38. Elijah, by ravens was fed,
   When told by the Lord where to hide;
 Some mornings they brought flesh and bread;
   And sometimes, in the eventide.

* Exod. xv. 11.   † Psa. l. 22.

A famine the Lord did command,
   And sent him to hide by a brook.
Baal's priests then reign'd in the land,
   And most the true worship forsook.

He had no communion with men,
   For none, it seems, knew he was there;
But angels did visit him then,
   And th' prophet was under their care.

The prophets of God had been slain,
   While many His service disown;
Idol-worship's established again,
   And th' evil had shamefully grown.

King Ahab, by Jezebel taught,
   Had sent to all nations around;
Long time for Elijah they sought,
   But nowhere was he to be found.

By her priests she had him possess'd,
   That he who had prophesied dearth,
By some evil th' nation distress'd,
   And brought down the curse on the earth.

So dark and benighted have been
   The dupes by false teachers deceiv'd:
As in ages past, such are seen
   To have all kinds of error believ'd.

In time the brook Cherith had dried,
   And th' prophet, directed elsewhere,
His new habitation he tried,
   And found a safe asylum there.

A handful of meal so increas'd,
   As daily to yield them a store!
The oil in the cruse had not ceas'd,
   Till th' days of the dearth had pass'd o'er!

He then was commanded to show
   Himself unto Ahab the king;
The hearts of the people to bow,
   And back to the true worship bring.

Baal's prophets were provèd and slain,
  The rain on the earth was then sent;
True religion established again,
  And th' people towards it intent.

The Lord seven thousand had known,
  And these had been sowing in tears:
To them, now, His favor is shown,
  And their God, th' true Saviour, appears.

ELIJAH'S TRANSLATION! L. M.
2 Kings ii. 9—15.

39. Elijah taken up to heaven,
  Was by a mighty whirlwind raised;
The sight was to Elisha given,
  But soon the holy vision ceased.

"My Father," twice the prophet cried,
  "The chariot and th' horsemen too,"
As he their fiery movement spied,
  "By which the sons of Israel go!"

To him Elijah's mantle fell,
  As he his garment rent in twain:
His spirit then did on him dwell,
  Yea, in a twofold power remain!

This certainly the prophet knew
  When straight he saw, with *inward* eyes.
The chariot which Elijah drew
  With whirling speed toward the skies

From this great sight he now return'd:
  And miracles, he too perform'd.
The minor prophets of him learn'd,
  Who then in companies were form'd.

Thus, though the prophets call'd to leave
  The few who may their loss bewail,
Others the Spirit still receive,
  For Israel's help can never fail.

D

ELIJAH'S TRANSLATION! S's.

2 Kings ii. 9—15.

40. To heaven, Elijah was borne
    By chariot and horses of fire,
 When he from Elisha was torn,
    And carried with speed through the air.

 How holy the joy which he felt,
    How weighty and glorious the bliss,
 Who knew the same spirit which dwelt
    On Elijah, was doubly his!

 From th' sight he returned in full power;
    By that power he miracles wrought,
 Which did his acceptance secure,
    For th' prophets all unto him sought.

 Thus, as it was then it is now,
    If any like him to truth cleave,
 And God does the Spirit bestow,
    His servants all such will receive.

"THE CHARIOT OF ISRAEL AND THE HORSEMEN THEREOF!" S's.

2 Kings ii. 12.

41. Th' chariot of Israel is love,
    Th' chariot of Israel is fire,
 This chariot more fleetly can move,
    Than whirlwinds that cut through the air.

 Its horsemen are lighter than flames,
    Its horses much swifter than hinds,
 How pure and immortal their beams,
    Flying on the wings of the winds!

 This chariot, so holy and fair,
    So bright and so comely to view,
 Which ages could never impair,
    Continueth ever as new.

Israel, who its service require,
    And a meetness for paradise prove,
Shall go in this chariot of fire,
    Shall go in this chariot of love!

This chariot is always prepared,
    To carry their spirits above,
To glory's exceeding reward,
    To reign in the Kingdom of love!

They die in the Lord, and are blest
    Through th' round of all ages to come
For ever and ever they rest,
    In th' heaven of heavens, their home.

THE SIEGE OF SAMARIA. L.M.

2 Kings vi. 24, &c.; vii. 1, &c.

42. Samaria of old, besieged
    Till all provision was subdued;
The din of war still round them raged,
    And famine, want and death ensued.

Then old Elisha prophesied,
    And sudden plenty he foretold,
Which was immediately supplied,
    And as he said, was cheaply sold.

Th' besiegers, God had made to hear
    A noise like armies leagued for war,
When they arose and fled for fear
    Of hired warriors from afar.

In their confusion and their haste,
    They left their *tents* in full display,
Garments and vessels from them cast,
    That they might faster get away!

Elisha's words seem'd strange to them:
    When they his prophecy had heard,
Its truth impossible did seem,
    And only vain surmisings stirr'd.

One spake of windows made on high,
　　If such a thing their eyes might see,
But thought not of th' Syrians nigh,
　　Nor how the Lord could make them flee.

The king, still harder to believe,
　　When he was told the host had fled,
Declared their *feint* was to deceive,
　　And catch them while in quest of bread!

But when he sent to search the way
　　With clothes and vessels thickly spread,
Then he no longer could gainsay,
　　But found it as the prophet said.

How hard are mortals to believe,
　　What with their eyes they cannot see,
How slowly they the truth receive,
　　By which souls live and are made free.

The Lord must sight and sense supply,
　　Before we trust His spoken words:
With grace from Him we then rely
　　On what His arm of power affords!

THE CHILD OF SORROW! C.M.

1 Chron. iv. 9, 10.

43. Jabez, a child of sorrow born,
　　Who in affliction came :
Expressive of a state forlorn,
　　Therefore a proper name.

As Jabez was a man of prayer,
　　And seriously inclined,
It shows he was in heart sincere,
　　And spiritual in mind.

He pray'd to God that He would bless,
　　And him from evil keep,
That he might larger coast possess
　　For cattle and for sheep.

And as the child of sorrow he
　　Would over evil grieve,
That God would his preserver be,
　　Who did his prayer receive.

In ev'ry thing he asked aright,
　　God granted his request,
Who in His children takes delight,
　　And gives them what is best!

Unto His sons upon the earth
　　All needful good is giv'n,
And as they are of higher birth,
　　The higher good in heav'n.

THE CHILD OF SORROW! 4-6s & 2-8s.

1 Chron. iv. 9, 10.

44. Jabez, a humble child,
　　　In grief and sorrow born,
　　He was in spirit mild,
　　　In habit taciturn;
And one, the most upright was he
Of all his tribe or family.

　　More hon'rable than they,
　　　In friendship more sincere,
　　Did all just laws obey,
　　　And was a man of prayer;
A fair example to the rest,
As in his walk and practice best!

　　He sought God's blessing most;
　　　Also that He would keep,
　　And give him larger coast
　　　For cattle and for sheep;
That God would him from evil save,
And he less grief and trouble have.

God his petition heard,
    And granted his request,
His constant friend appear'd,
    And gave him quiet rest;
To him good things on earth were giv'n,
And also better things in heav'n.

THE WELL OF BETHLEHEM!

1 Chron. xi. 15—19; 1 Sam. xx. 6.

45. David, like other warriors, had
    Of losses great to tell,
But for one loss he felt quite sad,
    The loss of Beth-l'hem's well.

David, then in the rock remained,
    Where many to him fell,
In its strong holds his post maintained,
    But thought of Beth-l'hem's well.

He thinks of home in early days,
    And where his kindred dwell,
But still one great concern betrays,
    It was for Beth-l'hem's well.

At length, he victory obtains,
    Did his proud foes expel,
And with a shout of joy regains
    The long sought Beth-l'hem's well!

Then would not David be the first,
    Who felt its sacred spell,
To satisfy and quench his thirst,
    At ancient Beth-l'hem's well?

And in the ages yet to come,
    The history shall tell,
Of David and his father's home,
    The place of Beth-l'hem's well.

THE TYPE AND ANTITYPE!

1 Chron. xi. 15—19.

46. The noted well of Beth-lehem,
　　　Instruction will afford,
　And with its ancient town proclaim,
　　　A lesson from the Lord.

　The town a high memorial has,
　　　As scripture doth declare;
　It the birth-place of David was,*
　　　And Jesus was born there.

　Its well was then a sacred type,
　　　And did most plainly tell,
　Of Jesus, the great Antitype,
　　　Of Christ, the living well!

　Men of the first might often drink,†
　　　Yet thirst and feel its pain,
　But he that doth of Jesus drink,
　　　Will never thirst again!

　For all that do in heart believe,
　　　And feel the Saviour there,
　Will water from their wells receive,
　　　Which living waters are.

　From Him, the living waters flow,
　　　Which He will freely give,
　This all His faithful follow'rs know,
　　　Who ever drink and live.

* Ruth i. 19 & ii. 4; 1 Sam. xx. 6; Matt. ii. 1.
† John iv. 13, 14.

THE CHARACTER OF JOB. 4-6's & 2-8's.

Job i. 1—8.

47. Upright was holy Job,
    And perfect in his day;
His character they rob,
    That otherwise would say:
He in his generation stood,
Approvèd and beloved of God.

    He greatly feared the Lord,
      And he served Him aright,
    While evil he abhorr'd,
      And chased it from his sight.
The poor in him a father had,
He made the wise and humble glad.

    Though in affliction great,
      Which sunk him very low,
    Some passages we meet,
      Which human weakness show:
Let others who may scoff at this,
Look home, where greater failing is.

    If Job was then reproved,
      For some things which he said,
    Those more from truth removed,
      Have cause to be afraid:
For He whose judgment is prepar'd,
To persons payeth no regard.

    And if the best of men,
      The wisest that have lived,
    (Job and his friends) are seen
      The Spirit to have grieved,
Instead of waiting on the Lord,
To speak according to His Word,

Let others warning take,
  By this example given,
Lest they also forsake
  Him who now speaks from heav'n,
In anything they do or say,
And from the path of duty stray.

Although you are the Lord's,
  And know His saving love,
Should you add to His words,
  He surely will reprove.
Thus you incur displeasure too,
In what you wrongly speak and do.

And in His judgment day,
  Which by His light is known,
Whate'er we do or say,
  It's clearly to us shown
Whether we are approved or blam'd,
Are justified or are condemn'd.

THE MISERY OF MAN'S FALLEN STATE.

Job v. 7.

48. Mankind unto trouble are born,
  As the sparks from a fire ascend ;
In vain our sad state do we mourn,
  If nothing but death will it end.

From the time sin entered man's heart,
  And induced his departure from God,
He has felt the sharp ling'ring smart,
  Of th' Almighty's chastening rod.

When man was created at first,
  Immortality shone on his brow ;
He neither knew hunger nor thirst,
  Nor sickness nor pain did he know'

He holy and innocent stood,
  Surrounded with bright scenes of love :
In possession of ev'ry good,
  And honored with guests from above !

But sin has beclouded that state
  Of honor, and glory, and bliss ;
And appointed to man a sad fate,
  Affliction and unhappiness.

No remedy then for this ill,
  While sin is permitted to reign ;
Afflictions abide ever will,
  Till new life shall ascendancy gain.*

Yet Jesus our sin can remove,
  Change th' nature we bring from the womb ;
The source of true happiness prove,
  And smooth the rough path to the tomb.

He is the true fountain of bliss,
  And if we in Him do believe,
True happiness we shall possess,
  And the life of eternity live.

THE SPEED OF TIME ! C.M.

Job vii. 6 & ix. 25, 26.

49. Our time is ever on the wing,
    Nor will it for us stay ;
  Each coming moment word will bring,
    That one is passed away.

  Moments continually are gone,
    And will return no more ;
  And if their work was then undone,
    Man must the loss endure.

* Rev. xxi. 3—4.

How swift are moments in their flight,
  How rapidly they move;
They steal away from mortal's sight,
  And thus their blindness prove.

As one succeeds another's haste,
  They still unmindful are:
And heedless let them " run to waste,"
  Without redeeming care.*

They do not see their value great,
  Nor improve on that account:
Thus while their courses they repeat,
  They to man's loss amount.

Hence may we with intention see,
  How valuable they are;
Nor unwisely suffer them to flee,
  Without improving care.

THE SHORTNESS AND UNCERTAINTY OF HUMAN LIFE. L.M.

Job xiv. 1—2.

50. Man who is of a woman born,
  How very sad and few his days!
Just like the blooming flower of morn,
  Cut down before the sun decays;

Or like a shadow on the ground,
  Which scarcely by the eye is seen,
And presently no more is found,
  But vanish'd from the sight of men.

Just as a post that swiftly flies,
  And hastens to its destined place,
So man speeds through his day and dies,
  And quickly ends his mortal race.

* Eph. v. 16.

Yet man he walks in a vain show,
    And is disquieted in vain,
While at his best estate doth know
    But vanity, and toil, and pain.

O may we so number our days,
    That we might hence apply our hearts
Only to walk in wisdom's ways,
    And learn the lessons she imparts.

For she will make us wise and blest,
    And to our waiting minds restore
The knowledge of eternal rest,
    And crown with glory evermore.

DEATH THE KING OF TERRORS!   8's.

Job xviii. 14.

51. Thou king of all terrors to man,
    Thou pale-visaged monster, grim Death!
Who windeth his days to a span,
    And holdest in awe all that breathe.

What scenes of fresh sorrow we meet,
    As thy chariot speeds on its way,
While thousands lie down at thy feet,
    Or fall to thy arrows a prey.

Thou smitest the old and the young,
    The poorest and richest by birth;
Thou slayest the weak and the strong,
    And all that are found on the earth.

For ages and ages gone by,
    Thy wars have been waged with all men,
And swift as thy summonses fly,
    Thy unfailing conquests have been.

JOB A BELIEVER IN THE RESURRECTION! L.M.

Job xix. 25—27.

52. I know that my Redeemer lives,
 And though the earth beneath the sod
This mortal body it receives,
 Yet for myself I shall see God.

For in the latter day, on earth,
 When He, in power, shall come again
To wake the dead and call them forth,
 That saints with Him may live and reign!

Then I shall my Redeemer see,
 Him and no other Saviour own,
From sin and death who will set free,
 And His own work with mercy crown.

And, as the living among men
 Know the corrections of His rod,
So they will see and praise Him then,
 The holy, true, and righteous God!

JOB'S LAMENTATION. S.M.

Job xxix. 2—6.

53. Oh that it were with me,
 As in months now pass'd o'er,
That God, as then, my trust would be,
 My guardian and my tower.

When His candle did shine
 Secretly on my head,
And His pure *inward light* divine
 Did me through darkness lead.

When in those times of love,
 And seasons of His grace,
The secret of my God above,
 Was on my dwelling-place!

Plenty was at my steps,
  Blessings did overflow :
But now mine eye with sorrow weeps,
  And none their pity show!

I mourn without the sun,*
  Like dragons of the deep,
Or like the owls, by day unknown
  Are heard when mortals sleep.

Oh, would the Lord in love,
  Again appear for me :
My burden and reproach remove,
  And my salvation be.

Would He reveal His power,
  And grant me a release :
His name again should be my tower,
  And this affliction cease.

Beneath His smiles of bliss,
  All trouble is unknown ;
He'll be my strength and righteousness,
  My glory and my crown!

"WHO TEACHETH LIKE HIM?"

Job xxxvi. 22.

54. If God himself our teacher is,
    We highly favored are ;
  No human teachings are like His,
    Nor may with His compare.

  More understanding He will give,
    Than earthly teachers can,
  If we alone unto Him live,
    And cease to trust in man!

* Job xxx. 28, 29.

He makes us know more than the beast,*
    Who seeking for their prey,
Both from the greatest to the least,
    True principles obey!

More than the fowls He will us show,
    Which come and go away;
And which their times and seasons know!
    If not the very day!

Wiser than all things sure are they,
    Who both with heart and will,
Their heav'nly Teacher's laws obey,
    And His commands fulfil.

A teacher of all truth is He,
    By spirit and by word;
The shepherd of His sheep will be,
    Their Saviour and their Lord.

THE FOOL!

Psa. xiv. 1.

55. The fool, who in his heart hath said,
    That there is not a God,
Has his foreboding fears and dread,
    As downward paths are trod.

While he rebels against the light,
    Walking the ways of sin,
The arrows of conviction smite,
    To turn him back again.

His guilty conscience feels the stings,
    Which spoil his fancied rest;
And busy mem'ry often brings,
    His courage to the test.

* Job xxxv. 11.

As he the way of life forsakes,
  His future is all gloom ;
While death a coward of him makes,
  Foreshadowing his doom.

All things below and all above,*
  Where'er he turns his eyes,
In ev'ry needful way will prove
  The truth which he denies !

That God who is Almighty lives,
  Is plainly understood :
As all creation witness gives,
  For Him the living God.

HEAVENLY FELICITY.

Psa. xvi. 11.

56. In the presence of God
    There is fulness of joy :
It's for ever bestow'd,
    Yet never will cloy.

And at His right hand,
    The hand of His power !
Where saints in light stand,
    Pleasures evermore !

Lord, may I partake
    Of bliss so divine :
For thy mercy's sake,
    With all that are Thine.

And then I for ever,
    Most blessed shall be ;
And praise the Great Giver,
    Of all unto me.

* Rom. i. 19, 20.

GOD'S WORKS AND PEOPLE PRAISE HIM.
Psa. xix. 1—6, and cxlv. 10, 11.　　　S. M.

57. The firmament on high
　　Sheweth the works of God,
And with the wonders they supply,
　　Proclaims His power abroad.

　　The spacious worlds above,
　　Arrayed in heav'nly light,
Are objects of His care and love,
　　And glorious in His sight.

　　How great must be the Lord,
　　The whole creation's trust;
How vast the wisdom of His Word,
　　Who made the whole at first!

　　No songs or notes we raise,
　　Could ever speak His fame,
Nor equal in the acts of praise,
　　The honors of his name.

THE WORKS OF GOD ARE GREAT AND GLORIOUS!
Psa. xix. 1—6, and civ. 24.　　　S. M.

58. Great are the works of God,
　　The wonders He hath wrought;
By Him the heav'ns were stretched abroad,
　　And to perfection brought.

　　He 'appointed day and night,
　　By His unerring skill;
The greater and the lesser light,
　　Make known His sov'reign will.

　　The num'rous stars above,
　　His handy works they are,
And those that in their courses move,
　　His wisdom will declare.

The earth with all therein,
  Was planted by His power;
He made the num'rous drops of rain,
  He gives the fruitful shower.

All perfect knowledge show,
  And wisdom infinite,
Which no created mind could know,
  Nor ever fathom it.

Yet all His works declare,
  His mercy and His love;
May we who in His favors share,
  In His blest service move.

THE SIN-SICK SOUL PRAYING FOR PARDON AND RESTORATION.

Psa. xxv. 11, 18.   L. M.

59. O Thou that hear'st the sinner's prayer,
Unto my mournful cry give ear,
And mercifully set me free,
From sin's disturbing malady.

With trembling voice I Thee invoke,
Upon my misery to look,
Behold me toil, with grief opprest,
And give the heavy laden rest.

Oh, grant the much desired release,
And heal my inward sicknesses,
The foul diseases of my soul,
And make my wounded spirit whole.

Now, Lord, a real soundness give,
Perfectly cure and let me live
In righteousness to see Thy face,
And realise absolving grace.

THE PENITENT'S PRAYER AND HOPE IN THE MERCY OF GOD.

Psa. xxv. 16—18; Micah. vii. 18. 7's and 6's.

60. Press'd with sin and sorrow's weight,
   Feeling the burden sore,
In the watches of the night,
   My mis'ry I deplore.
As forsaken by my hope,
   Of th' smiling day's return,
Midst the darkness do I grope,
   And inwardly I mourn.

Oh, Thou God of mercy, hear,
   And pity one distrest,
Shed on me compassion's tear,
   And give the weary rest.
Quiet make the troubled sea,
   For confusion doth me fill,
Hear the humbled sinner's plea,
   And answer, Peace, be still!

Surely now fresh hope I have,
   The dawn of day begins,
Thou wilt ransom from the grave,
   And save me from my sins.
Thou wilt me Thy mercy show,
   In love my soul upraise,
I shall Thy salvation know,
   And Thee for ever praise.

PRAISE FOR DELIVERANCE FROM DANGER.

Psa. xxxiv. 1—8. S. M.

61. I'll praise the Lord always,
   And thanks to Him will give,
For all the goodness He displays
   And mercies I receive.

I'll lean upon His word,
  And trust Him for His grace,
By which He doth His help afford,
  In ev'ry time and place.

O magnify with me
  Our good and gracious God;
Let Him alone exalted be,
  Whose favors are bestow'd.

When poor and much distress'd,
  I unto Him had cried,
He me from all my fears releas'd,
  And all my wants supplied!

I will at all times bless
  And praise His holy name,
His providential acts confess,
  And thank Him for the same.

I'll praise Him while I live,
  For saving mercy given,
Who will at last my soul receive,
  To praise His name in heaven.

ENCOURAGEMENT TO THE AFFLICTED SERVANTS OF GOD.

Psa. xxxiv. 19.   C. M.

62. The righteous many trials have,
  Yet God delivereth them:
And He hath pledged Himself to save,
  Though all beside condemn.

Should all their enemies combine
  To tread them in the dust,
Still let them not His paths decline,
  Nor yet withdraw their trust.

The fight of faith is glorious,
　　Immortal its renown,
And Jesus will o'ercome for us;
　　Through Him we wear the crown!

The crown of life and victory
　　He will the faithful give,
Which they shall wear eternally
　　And ever with Him live.

CONFIDENCE IN GOD, THE SAVIOUR OF THOSE THAT PUT THEIR TRUST IN HIM

Psa. xxxvii. 39, 40.

63. The Lord is my deliverer,
　　I will not be afraid,
For where I am my God is there,
　　And with a present aid.

He keeps me with a watchful eye,
　　My safety does approve,
And manifests His presence nigh
　　By His all-constant love!

Through snares and traps my soul could go,
　　Nor death nor danger fear,
While Thee by faith and trust I know
　　So intimately near.

Thy hand protects me from my foes
　　By a commanding power,
And grace, which now before me goes,
　　Will save me evermore.

ENCOURAGEMENT TO TRUST IN GOD.

Psa. xlii. 5, 11.　　　　　7's.

64. Why art thou cast down, my soul?
　　Why art thou disquieted?
　Christ will all thy foes control
　　Who for thee His blood hath shed.

　Give no place to doubt or fear,
　　Though He seem to hide His face,
　He most surely will appear
　　In the power of saving grace!

　Then believe, be bold, be strong;
　　Rest, still hoping in the Lord;
　Though He seem to tarry long,
　　Ever faithful is His word.

　Look, my soul, to Him and prove
　　That His promises are sure;
　Plead His mercy and His love,
　　Trust Him now and evermore.

"A SONG OF LOVES!"

Psa. xlv. 1—6.　　　　　L. M.

65. My heart good matter will indite,
　My hand, with ready pen will write,
　If grace shall holy fervor bring,
　To speak of things touching the King.

　More fair than are the sons of men,
　More lovely is the Saviour seen,
　And grace is pour'd into His lips,
　Who endless stores of blessing keeps!

Gird now Thy sword upon Thy thigh,
And in Thy glorious majesty
Ride on to prosper righteousness,
And sin and wickedness repress.

Thine arrows, they are sharp indeed,
Which make the heart and conscience bleed,
And pointed by unerring aim,
Thy mighty conquests will proclaim.

Thine enemies, both near and far,
Who are made captives in the war,
Will willingly to Thee submit,
And sue for mercy at Thy feet!

The words of pardon from Thy mouth
Are words of everlasting truth;
Thy sceptre and Thy throne is sure,
And will for evermore endure.

"A SONG OF LOVES!"

Psa. xlv. 1—7.   L. M.

66. My heart a good theme shall indite,
My hand with ready pen shall write,
If grace shall inspiration bring,
To speak the honors of the King.

Fairer than any sons of men
Is Christ the holy Saviour seen,
And grace is pour'd into His lips,
Who stores of ev'ry blessing keeps!

Anointed over all as Head,
His royal dignity hath spread,
And nations hearing of His fame,
Will bow before His mighty name!

In majesty, exalted high,
Gird now Thy sword upon Thy thigh,
Ride on to war in righteousness,
And sin and wickedness repress.

Thy sword is sharp, Thine arrows keen,
Whereby Thine enemies are seen
As rebels falling at Thy feet,
That they may pard'ning mercy meet!

The words proceeding from Thy mouth
Are words of everlasting truth;
Thy sceptre and Thy kingdom's sure,
And will eternally endure.

PRAISE FOR PROVIDENTIAL MERCIES.

Psa. lix. 16, 17.   L. M.

67. Awake, my soul, a grateful lay,
This morning of another day;
The tribute of thy praises bring
Unto thy Saviour, God and King.

In humble thanks, lift up thy voice,
And in His holy name rejoice,
Who gives thee strength and grace each day,
To walk uprightly in His way.

When evils have beset my path,
His providential goodness hath
In dangers both unseen and seen,
To me a sure protection been.

He holds me by His arm of pow'r,
And saves me in temptation's hour,
So that my footsteps do not slide,
Nor from His way-marks turn aside.

His hands with blessings richly stor'd,
Supplies for all my wants afford,
And all I am, and all I have,
He graciously in goodness gave.

I'll thank and praise Him in my song,
To whom all thanks and praise belong,
Whose grace and goodness will endure
In faithfulness for evermore.

GOD'S POWER OVER HIS ENEMIES.

Psa. lxviii. 1, 2, 18.　　　　　S. M.

68. Let God in strength arise,
 That men Thy hand may see,
To scatter all Thy enemies,
 And make them fear or flee.

 As smoke is driv'n away,
 So drive them by Thy power,
'Till they shall down their weapons lay,
 And dare rebel no more.

 As wax melteth in fire
 And burns till it consume,
Let all their ill designs expire
 And like to it become.

 By terror and by grace
 The bold transgressors meet,
Subdue, and melt the rebel race,
 And bring them to Thy feet.

 They will to Thee submit
 Soon as their power is gone,
When conquer'd they will lowly sit,
 And bow to Thee alone.

So shall Thy vict'ries spread,
  Extending more and more,
And sinners who are captives led
  Shall join to praise Thy power.

THE SOLEMNITY OF DEATH.

Psa. lxxxix. 48; Job xiv. 10, 12.   S. M.

69. How solemn is the thought
  That I must surely die,
And be as others long forgot,
  Who without mem'ry lie.

In the cold darksome grave
  This body must be laid,
The dreary home which all must have,
  And join the sleeping dead.

Our mould'ring dust will there
  In ceaseless slumbers lay,
And man's mortality declare
  Until the judgment day,

When we must rise again,
  And shall immortal be,
Yea, in a deathless state remain
  To all eternity!

True bliss or misery
  In endless state to prove,
Shut out from God eternally,
  Or live with Him above.

THE SHORTNESS AND UNCERTAINTY OF HUMAN LIFE.

Psa. xc. 3—10.   4—6's and 2—8's.

70. Alas, our mortal state,
  How very sad its fate;
How soon our health and strength decays,
  And we return to dust,
  From whence we sprang at first,
And finish these our mournful days.

Mortals are like to grass,
So swift their time they pass,
And as a shadow flee away;
As op'ning flowers they shine,
Then speedily decline,
And the just debt of nature pay.

Is threescore years and ten
Allotted unto men
While on their trial here below?
Then if they reach fourscore
Their burden will be sore,
And greater travail will they know.

Our years they glide along
Much like unto a song,
Or to a tale that soon is told:
So short on earth our stay,
So soon we fly away,
And yet how firm is nature's hold!

Look how we grovel here,
How full of toil and care,
As if it were our only home;
How seldom do we strive,
Above the world to live,
Against the day of wrath to come.

That day approaches fast,
And God requires the past,
If we in sinful ways have gone;
Of Him we must receive,
However we may live,
According to our works now done.

Moses, in this Psalm, does not fix the limit of human life generally to 70 or 80 years. Caleb was as strong and able for war at 85* as he was at 40. Joshua lived 110 years; Moses 120; and Aaron 123. The pas-

*Josh. xiv. 10, 11, and xxiv. 29. Num. xxxiii. 39. Deu. xxxiv. 7.

sage, strictly understood, applied to those Israelites who had sinned, and were doomed by God to die in the wilderness. Examples could be given of persons recently deceased who lived to be a 100 or more than 100 years of age. The longest life is short in comparison of the lives of the Antediluvians, and divine prophecy furnishes ground for believing that the ages of men will be increased before the end of the world to the ages of men before the flood, some of whom lived nearly 1,000 years.—Isa. lxv. 20—22.

PRAISE FOR AFFLICTION.

"I WILL SING OF MERCY AND JUDGMENT."

Psa. ci. 1. C. M.

71. Father, how kind Thy dealings are,
  How great Thy mercies prove;
How watchful is Thy tender care,
  How melting is Thy love!

Thou dost chastise Thy favor'd sons,
  Who in wrong ways have trod,
And then in pity to their groans,
  Withdraw'st Thy gentle rod.

Thy saving love and power to show,
  Is the affliction sent,
And though it grieves and sinks them low,
  Is still in kindness meant!

For that which humbles comes to woo
  And bind our spirits fast;
Then we may sing of mercy too,
  And know the judgment past!

PRAISE FOR ALL MERCIES.
Psa. ciii. 1—5. S. M.

72. O bless the Lord, my soul,
   And praise His holy name,
Whose grace thy wand'rings did control,
   Thy waywardness o'ercame.

   Who forgiveth thy sins,
   Who heals thy sicknesses,
And by His power thy life sustains
   In loving faithfulness!

   He fills thy mouth with good,
   Doth renewed strength supply,
As eagles with their feathered brood,
   When teaching them to fly.*

   His arm doth me embrace,
   He saveth me from ill,
And by the lessons of His grace,
   Makes me to know His will!

   His benefits are great,
   For they unnumber'd are,
No tongue His mercies can repeat,
   Nor their extent declare.

   I'll praise Him as the Word,†
   While on the earth I live,
And in the Kingdom of the Lord,
   Eternal praises give.

THE UNCERTAINTY OF LIFE.
Psa. ciii. 15, 16. C. M.

73. Death hurries all its sons to dust,
   It brings the mighty down,
Ourselves a day we cannot trust,
   Nor call an hour our own.

* Ex. xix. 4; Deu. xxxii. 11, 12.   † John 1. 1.

Yet men through blindness dwell secure,
   They many schemes will start,
And when they deem success as sure,
   May suddenly depart.

Daily we see our kindred die,
   And turn again to dust,
Where millions long forgotten lie,
   With ev'ry mem'ry lost.

Nor are we safe, no more than they
   Which daily close their breath;
Shortly the call we must obey,
   And clasp the arms of death.

Death comes to all, with speed of flight
   It hurries men away,
Who quickly pass to endless night,*
   Or everlasting day.

Merciful God, prepare us all
   For glory, where Thou art,
That whensoe'er Thy wisdom call,
   We may in peace depart.

THE GODHEAD AND ETERNAL DIVINITY OF THE LORD JESUS CHRIST ENTITLING HIM TO ALL HOMAGE AND PRAISE!

Psa. ciii. 19—22.　　Col. i. 15—17.　　S. M.

74. Praise ye the heav'nly King,
   The true incarnate one,
Let all an humble tribute bring,
   And worship at His throne.

How holy is His seat,
   How righteous all His ways,
And oh, how glorious and great,
   The sceptre which He sways!

* Psa. xlix. 19, see margin.

Angels obey His word,
  They on His pleasure wait,
To Jesus, their Almighty Lord,
  They cheerfully submit:

Swift in their courses move,
  His orders to fulfil,
And lured by His transcendent love,
  Delight to do His will!

Let Rulers learn the same,*
  And thankfully esteem,
In due submission to His name,
  Their services to Him.

Their service is His due,
  And what Himself enjoin'd,
Whose high commands are just and true,
  And should all people bind.

For worthy is the Son,
  All honors to receive,
In union with the Father one,
  Eternally to live.

Let earth with all its tongues,
  Her purest off'rings raise,
To whom the privilege belongs,
  To celebrate His praise.

THE TRUE LIGHT TO PURITY AND SALVATION.

Psa. cxix. 9.   L. M.

75. How shall a young man cleanse his way?
  By taking heed unto Thy Word,
Who will instruct him day by day,
  And ev'ry needful help afford.

* Psa. ii. 10, 12.

The inward Word of life we mean, *
   He who alone the soul can save,
By whom it must be born again, †
   And ransomed from a yawning grave.

This Word is nigh, yea, in thy heart, ‡
   The Word of faith, the Word of grace,
Nor will it from thy mouth depart,
   Long as it there can find a place.

This is the living Word of God, §
   The Word of His salvation too,
Which was made flesh, and shed His blood,
   To save mankind from sin and woe!

For He alone can save the lost,
   Who hath His Spirit freely giv'n,
Oh, then to Him thy guidance trust,
   And learn of Him who speaks from heav'n!

He'll be a light unto thy feet, ‖
   A lantern to thy path will prove,
And through obedience make thee meet,
   To dwell in Paradise above!

QUICKENING GRACE INVOKED.

Psa. cxix. 25.   S. M.

76. Quicken my soul, O Lord,
   Which cleaveth to the dust;
Upraise me by thy pow'rful Word,
   Who in Thy mercy trust.

For Thy life-giving Word
   My soul hath waited long,
His presence doth new light afford,
   His love a pleasant song.

---

* Jas. i. 21.   † 1 Pet. i. 23—25.   ‡ Rom. x. 6—10.
§ Heb. iv. 12—14; John i. 1—4, 14.   ‖ Psa. cxix. 105.

When His bright beams I see,
  I'm ravished with the bliss:
My soul is then from evil free,
  And fill'd with joy and peace.

In this delightful frame
  My happy soul would rest,
To see, and love, and praise Thy name,
  And be for ever blest.

DELIGHT IN THE LAW OF GOD.
Psa. cxix. 97—100. S. M.

77. Lord, how I love Thy law,
  It is my chief delight:
By day I thence instruction draw,
  And comfort in the night.

How perfect and how good,
  How righteous and how pure,
Thy statutes seem when understood,
  And all Thy precepts sure.

Oh, may I never stray
  From light so freely giv'n,
Nor miss Thy pointings of the way
  Which lead the soul to heav'n—

The heav'n of light and love
  In which the Angels dwell,
Who, in Thy holy service move,
  And all Thy praises tell.

THE LOVE OF GOD'S LAW THE SOURCE OF TRUE PEACE.
Psa. cxix. 165. C. M.

78. Great peace have they that love Thy law,
  The precepts of Thy mouth;
Thence they delightful lessons draw,
  And learn the ways of truth.

They know the truth, O God, indeed,
    And thus are they made free,
And with alacrity and speed
    Direct their steps to Thee.

Their services are made divine,
    Such as Thou dost approve,
Their body, soul and spirit Thine,
    The purchase of Thy love!

Through Jesus' justifying blood
    They know their sins forgiv'n,
And, when they die, will live with God
    Eternally in heav'n!

PROSPERITY AND SAFETY ARE OF THE LORD.

Psa. cxxvii. 1, 2.   L. M.

79. Except the Lord shall build the house,
    They labor but in vain that build;
And all who shall the work espouse,
    Will fruitlessly their labors yield.

Except the Lord the city keep,
    The watchman waketh but in vain,
He might as well securely sleep
    Free from his anxious toil and pain.

O Thou on whom our help is laid,
    By whom we from our cares are freed,
On whom alone our hope is stay'd,
    Be Thou our friend in time of need.

Grant us good speed in Thy great name
    Until the building finished be,
And safely keep and guard the same
    For us and our posterity.

THE MAJESTY AND GLORY OF GOD'S KINGDOM!

Psa. cxlv. 10—13.

80. The Monarch that rules in heav'n,
    The high and the lofty One,
To Him all praises are giv'n
    By the angels round His throne.

The Seraphim, they will raise
    Their voices in worship pure;
The Cherubim, they will praise
    Him who reigns for evermore.

His majesty and kingdom,
    How glorious to behold:
His 'mazing pow'r and wisdom
    Where His wonders all unfold!

Though high His habitation,
    He not only dwelleth there,
He knows no limitation,
    For He is everywhere!

Vast source of infinity
    From Thy hand all being came!
Great King of eternity
    We give honor to Thy name.

We, who Thy grace possessing,
    Are favor'd to know Thy way,
Will give Thee thanks and blessing,
    And will praise Thee day by day.

We read in ancient story
    Thy wonders and deeds of yore,
And would praise th' Lord of glory
    Both now and for evermore.

THE DISPLAYS OF GOD'S POWER ON EARTH.
Psa. cxlvii. 5, 15—18. 7's.

81. God is great and of great power,
    And how great no tongue can tell,
Who doth send the frozen shower
    And confine the river's swell.

Like morsels He doth send ice,
    Or, like wool He sendeth snow,
And His south wind doth suffice
    To make streams and rivers flow.

He can slay with scorching heat!
    He can kill with piercing cold!
For in both His power is great,
    And how great cannot be told!

Who may dare resist His rod?
    Who may stand before His frown?
He is an avenging God,
    And can smite opponents down.

When His word He sendeth forth,
    It doth very swiftly run,
And, in all parts of the earth
    Where it flies, His will is done.

Then let all the tribes of men
    Bow submissive to His word,
All earth's changes, it is plain,
    Are appointed by the Lord.

HUMAN KINDNESS AND ITS FRUITS.
Prov. v. 15—17. 7's. & 6's.

82 Drink thine own waters flowing
    From cistern or from well,
Kindness to others showing,
    Who near to thee may dwell.

Let thy well be a blessing,
    Distributing to those
Whose wants may be most pressing,
    And facts such wants disclose.

Thy favors thus receiving,
    Of which they stand in need,
And in their minds reviving,
    May prompt a friendly deed.

Who seek a friendship rather
    Than care friendship to show,
Will just reproaches gather,
    And their ill name will grow.

Good actions deserve credit,
    At least, for good intent,
While evil actions merit
    A timely punishment.

THE SPIRIT OF DIVINE WISDOM REGENERATING SOULS FOR AN HABITATION.

Prov. viii. 1—4, 32—36.   C. M.

83. Hark, from the regions of the skies
    A soft descending voice,
She cheers her lovers as she flies,
    And makes their hearts rejoice.

She passes as the wind unseen, *
    And where succeeds her plan,
She mediates a peace between
    God and His creature man.

When by her scheme of righteousness
    She rests her heav'nly form,
She clothes again man's nakedness,
    And love adorns a worm.

* John iii. 7, 8.

As tabernacles such will stand,
　And marks of glory show,
Embellished by th' artistic hand,
　Which can no equal know.

Their ornament is heav'nly light,
　Decked with its costly rays,
Which are to all a goodly sight,
　That walk in wisdom's ways.

Grace spiritually a form bestows,
　Creating an abode
Which to a living temple grows,
　Inhabited by God!

DIVINE RETRIBUTION FOR NEGLECT OF THE POOR.

Pro. xxi. 13. 9's.

84. If the cry of the poor is not heard
　When it's press'd by affliction and need,
Inspiration hath plainly averr'd
　The hard-hearted shall pine for the deed.

For to persons God has no respect,
　Yet He pleadeth the cause of the poor,
And He will their petitions reject,
　Who to others have shut mercy's door!

But charities when rightly bestow'd
　On the children of want and distress,
Is most plainly commended of God, *
　And He who gives all blessings will bless!

His blessing, it makes rich on the earth,
　Is most freely and graciously given,
And will grow and increase in its worth
　To its highest fruition in heav'n!

* Psa. xli. 1, 2.

PRAYING FOR PARDON AND RECONCILIATION WITH GOD.

Pro. xxviii. 13.   4—6's. & 2—8's.

85. Pardon, O Lord, the crimes
Which I have oftentimes
In such a thoughtless manner done;
Committed in Thy sight,
Against the clearest light,
And from preserving mercy gone.

For this sinful abuse
I am without excuse,
So deeply do I feel condemned;
And if I underwent
Thy righteous punishment,
Myself alone were to be blamed.

Yet God in love we find
Compassionate and kind
To such as turn to Him from sin;
Although the most upright
Mercy is Thy delight,
As all Thy servants will maintain.

'Tis not Thy heav'nly will
That any one should fill
His measure of iniquities:
To feel beneath thy wrath
The bitterness of death,
With all its direful agonies.

Oh, let Thy Spirit then,
By a conviction keen,
Produce a penitential smart:
My evil passions slay,
Purge my foul guilt away,
And reconciling grace impart.

So shall I know the Lord
In deed as well as word,
And spread the knowledge all abroad,
That many who shall see
May hear and turn to thee,
Their great redeemer and their God.

THE BEAUTIES OF EARTH TYPICAL OF THE GLORIES IN HEAVEN!

"He hath made everything beautiful in his time."
Eccles. iii. 11. 9's.

86. In the beautiful blossoming earth
Is a figure of paradise seen!
In its lovely attraction and worth,
As it now and it ever hath been.

In this looking-glass we may behold
A reflection of glories above,
Though but weakly its beauties unfold,
Typing those in the kingdom of love!

And it may be instructive to know,
By the lessons of nature here given,
That the earth's brightest beauties will show,
As a mirror, those brighter in heaven!

Though but faintly we see in this glass,
What is presently fading away,
Yet we know, as their shadows may pass,
The immortal will never decay!

"THE LIVING KNOW THAT THEY SHALL DIE."

Eccles. ix. 5; Heb. ix. 27. C.M.

87. Death soon removes us out of time
Into eternity,
Some young, some old, some in their prime,
To fix their destiny.

What numbers are there ev'ry day
  Committed to the ground,
To mingle with their kindred clay,
  Where life no more is found.

Thousands innumerable are there,
  Who will be seen no more,
And all the common fate must share
  With those now gone before.

Mortals pass off life's stage in haste,
  And thence have disappear'd,
Each moment sees their numbers waste—
  By others still repair'd.

Some on the left, some on the right,
  By death are taken hence,
And who can match th' unequal fight, *
  Or make a safe defence ?

Death reigns a conqu'ror over all,
  None can his power withstand,
Princes and kings before him fall,
  They bow at his command.

Thus mortals on one level meet,
  Meet on one common line,
Laying their honors at his feet,
  Who leaves them to decline.

Beneath his all despotic sway,
  Which awes them to the dust,
Their glories hasten to decay,
  And are for ever lost !

THE PREACHER GIVING INSTRUCTION.
Eccles. ix. 7, 8.   8's.

88. May th' voice of the preacher be heard,
  Who giveth right counsel to men,
To listen may we be prepar'd,
  And take the advice of his pen.

* Eccles. viii. 8.

To go in the way that is right,
  The way which our Maker befriends,
To eat of His bread with delight,
  And drink of the wine which He sends!

The bread which true vigor imparts,
  By making fresh blood in our veins,
The good wine which cheereth our hearts,
  The wine which His blessing contains! *

May righteousness wait on our steps,
  And our garments always be white,
That the Lord who His children keeps,
  May us in His goodness requite.

In His mercy He blesseth our toil,
  And our labor is sooner forgot,
He anointeth our head with His oil,
  And gladness and joy is our lot!

At His table we feast on rich fare,
  And our souls they are fill'd with good,
As we in His services share,
  And life from His presence has flow'd.

THE PREACHER'S ADVICE.

Eccles. ix. 7, 8.   4—6's and 2—8's.

89. We hear the preacher say
  To man, Now go thy way
And eat thy daily bread with joy;
  The wine God doth impart,
  Take with a cheerful heart,
And in His cause thyself employ.

  Thy mind to Him unite,
  And keep thy garments white,
That on thy head His ointment pour'd
  May fill thy soul with joy:
  And all thy thoughts employ
To love and serve thy living Lord.

* Isa. lxv. 8.

EXPOSTULATION.
Eccles. xi. 9, 10.

90. Rejoice, O young man, in thy youth,
    And let thy heart cheer thee with mirth,
To despise th' examples of truth,
    And follow sin's pleasures on earth.

Go on in the sight of thine eyes,
    And walk in the ways of thine heart,
By serving the father of lies,
    And sharing his followers' part.

Forget the concerns of thy soul,
    Nor remember the hour of death,
Yea, please thy own self to the full,
    And store up the treasures of wrath.

Yet know this, that when all is past,
    When arrested thou art in thy course,
The sweet will be bitter at last,
    The joy will be turned to remorse.

And when thou art called to account,
    Though this warning thy reason disdains,
How great will appear the amount
    Of all thy presumptuous sins.

Shalt thou then be able to stand
    In th' presence of God, the great King,
When He thy defence shall demand,
    And all things to memory bring?

Will not all thy courage then fail,
    When wrath shall thy sentence proclaim,
And justice and judgment prevail,
    Unto thy confusion and shame?

Then take wisdom's counsel betimes, *
    And begin from this present day,
By forsaking all follies and crimes,
    To walk in life's happier way.

* Prov. i. 20—23, and ii. 10—19.

THE GLORIES OF CHRIST!

Cant. i. 2, 3, and ii. 1—4.   4—8's and 2—6's.

91. Sweet as the rose of Sharon's fields,
The lily of the valley yields
  Its scented fumes around ;
But Jesus' love them both exceeds :
The odours it so richly sheds
  Are more refreshing found !

Though to the rose of blooming air,
Or to the lily, spotless fair,
  His likeness is compar'd,
Yet still His beauties are displayed
Beyond an emblem or a shade,
  Which soon have disappear'd.

The brightest flowers that bloom on earth,
In all their elegance and worth,
  His hands alone have made :
Their tinted hues of various dye,
Their comeliness and purity,
  Before His glories fade !

What shall display Thy beauties then ?
Not flowers, that win the gaze of men;
  Things human nor divine.
Thy glories far exceed the best,
Are of undying charms possest,
  And ev'ry grace is Thine !

ADORATION.
Cant. i. 3. L. M.

92. Thy name, as ointment, is pour'd forth,
Which shows its saving pow'r and worth ;
Thy dove-like Spirit, gracious Lord,
Doth this anointing grace afford !

Thy people all to Thee are known,
Thy name is named on all Thine own,
And truth, and love, and holiness,
Doth well Thy living name express !

UNIVERSAL PEACE!
Isa. ii. 2—4; Micah iv. 1—4.

93. House of the Lord, exalted high
Above the hills, far off and nigh,
Upon the mountain of our God,
On which it has for ages stood.

When men the house of God shall know,*
And from their hills and mountains go,
That He may teach them His right way,
And they from Him no more may stray,

They evil courses will forsake,
And of destroying weapons make
Their useful implements of trade—
The plough, the sickle, and the spade.

Led by the hills and mountains seen,
Fightings and wars have always been;
But with His one religion pure
The nations will learn war no more!

The wars which men on earth have waged,
The laws of brotherhood outraged;
For as one family they are,
Each should the other's friendship share.

Thus men's false systems led astray,
But when God teaches all His way,
Then peace will reign on ev'ry shore,
And wars will cease and be no more!

"CEASE YE FROM MAN."
Isa. ii. 22.

94. Cease my soul to look to man,
On an arm of flesh to trust;
For no outward greatness can
Once recover sinners lost.

* Jer. iii. 23.

Of his wisdom make account
  Why I stoop to learn of him?
Foolishness is its amount*
  In thy Maker's just esteem.

For his knowledge reason make
  Why I should obey his words?
Man must all his own forsake †
  Ere the Saviour His affords.

In his preaching or his prayers,
  For his learning these esteem?
Jesus testimony bears
  All are nothing without Him! ‡

Cease from man, entirely cease,
  Who has nothing truly good;
Who himself the Lord to please,
  Must await His grace bestow'd.

Man as man may useful be,
  Yet in Christ his glories fade;
Cease from man, wherein is he ||
  Of account thus to be made!

PRAISE FOR THE NATIVITY AND SACRIFICIAL
WORK OF CHRIST.

Isa. vii. 14; Mat. i. 23; 1 Tim. iii. 16.   S. M.

95. Come tune a lofty strain
  To God the Saviour's name;
Thoughts of the past revive again
  When He as man became.

When He assumed our flesh,
  And veiled His glory there,
To show in miracles afresh
  How great His mercies are!

* 1 Cor. i. 20.   † 1 Cor. viii. 2.   ‡ John xv. 5. || 1 Cor. iii. 5, 7.

Jesus, as man and God,
  The Lord of life and power,
This lower world of mis'ry trod,
  And did proud scorn endure.

To degradation He
  Submitted here beneath;
Consented the despis'd to be,
  And yielded unto death.

Poverty and distress,
  Mark'd with her saddest gloom,
The mighty Maker did possess,
  That we might rich become!

Come speak aloud His praise—
  His unparallel'd love;
A song of pure thanksgiving raise
  Unto the Lord above.

With grateful heart and voice,
  Speak forth His worthy name;
In His unequall'd love rejoice,
  And celebrate the same.

Long as the world shall last,
  May Adam's ransomed race
Record the wondrous doings past,
  Of His unbounded grace!

THE ETERNAL DIVINITY OF JESUS CHRIST!

Isa. ix. 6; John i. 1—3.   S. M.

96. The Lord on high proclaims
  The titles of His Son,
And in His own appropriate names
  Makes the blest person known.

Jesus the Wonderful,
　The matchless Counsellor,
The mighty God, all powerful,
　The heav'nly Conqueror.*

Th' immortal Prince of Peace,
　The great and dreadful King,
The Father of Almighty grace,
　And God from everlasting!†

The only Potentate,‡
　The Lord of life and power,
Who did at first all things create,
　And reigns for evermore!

The righteous King of Kings,‖
　The Lord of Lords most High,
Whose pow'r alone upholds all things,
　Whose praise will never die.

Let worlds their homage pay,
　And at His footstool fall;
Who reigns with universal sway,
　The sovereign Lord of all!

THE TITLES AND PREROGATIVES OF CHRIST!
Isa. ix. 6—7. 7's & 6's.

97. Alpha and Omega, He,¶
　Beginning and the end,
King of kings eternally,
　And man's immortal friend!

He who a man-child was born,
　The Son of David giv'n;
He and whose exalted horn
　Shall rule in earth and heav'n.

* Rev. xix. 11, 13.　† Mic. v. 2.　‡ 1 Tim. vi. 14, 16.
‖ Rev. xix. 13, 16.　¶ Rev. xxii. 13.

Counsellor of counsel full,
  To those that trust in Him;
He whose name is wonderful
  To save and to redeem!

For He is the mighty God,
  The eternal Father, He
Who as man hath shed his blood,
  The Prince of Peace to be!

He in majesty sustains
  An undisputed throne;
He who now in glory reigns,
  And who will reign alone.

THE ENSIGNS OF CHRIST!

Isa. xi. 10, 12 & xviii. 3.   7's & 6's.

98. Christ is the great Prince of Peace,
      As witnessed at His birth;
    In His times all wars must cease
      Upon this fighting earth!

Though the Lion of the tribe*
  Of Judah's warlike name;
On His ensign see inscribed
  The gentle, peaceful Lamb!

As a lion in His day,†
  Of terror and renown,
He His enemies will slay,
  And tread their minions down.

He will all their forces fight
  Until he overcome,
And by His victorious might
  The government assume.

* Rev. v. 5, 6.   † Isa. xxxi. 4; Jer. xxv. 30.

Yet as Prince of Peace He reigns
  Over His Church below;
Thence His peaceful rule maintains,
  Which all the earth shall know!

Then the kingdoms of this world
  Shall bow before His name,
When His *ensigns* are unfurl'd—
  The Lion! and the Lamb!

A SONG OF SALVATION!
Isa. xii. 1—6.   4·6's & 2·8's.

99.   God's people will Him praise,
  When from their low estate
He shall their souls upraise,
  With life invigorate;
When from all yokes He makes them free,
And they shall their deliverer see.

He'll surely come for them,
  Although He tarry long:
With a strong arm redeem,
  And He will be their song.
When they shall know His promised word,
And find salvation in the Lord!

They keep His righteous law,
  Which ends all guilty strife;
And now with joy they draw
  Out of the wells of life,
The wells of His salvation known,
The living waters as their own.

They wholly serve the Lord,
  They trust alone in Him;
Obey the inward Word,*
  And His great pow'r proclaim:
The song of His salvation sing,
And spread the praises of their King.

* Jas. i. 21.

THE WELLS OF GOD'S SALVATION!
Isa. xii. 3.

100. We living waters draw with joy
  Out of the living wells;
The waters which will ne'er alloy,
  And whose source never fails.

In all the new-born souls around,
  For there the Saviour dwells,
The living waters may be found,
  Drawn from their living wells.

The wells of God's salvation these,
  Salvation by His Word;*
Whose never-failing springs increase,
  And light and joy afford.

We ask of Him, and He doth give
  The living water pure,
Of which we drink, by which we live,
  And know His promise sure.

Fountain of living waters He,†
  Supplying all our wells;
Whose trust alone in Him must be,
  As He Himself reveals.

Those waters never cease their swell,
  For all their springs are sure,
Supplying ev'ry living well,
  Both now and evermore.

THE FALL OF BABYLON:
Isa. xiii. 1—5.

101. Ye messengers of the most High,
  Who in His highness will rejoice,
Gather His chosen servants nigh;
  Yea, shake the hand, exalt the voice.

*Acts xiii. 26. †Jer. ii. 13 & xvii. 13.

For to command His sanctified,
   Now the great trumpet shall be blown:
With heav'nly arms and armour tried,
   Those mighty ones whom He hath known.

His banner on the mountain top,
   So that it may be seen from far,
Must now by you be lifted up,
   And the host mustered for the war.

Then be courageous for the Lord,
   To Him a willing service pay;
Hearken to the Almighty Word,*
   And fight your battles in His day!

Your great Commander and your Head
   Will all your enemies tread down;
Yea, He will forth His army lead,
   And them with certain vict'ry crown.

Like a great lion, saith the Lord,†
   Tearing and ravening the prey,
Which many shepherds won't regard,
   Nor for their shoutings turn away,

So will I be with you and fight,
   Till all my foes are overthrown;
And by my terror and my might,
   Will tread their pow'r and glory down.

They of the ensign are afraid,‡
   Which shall be seen from far by them;
Saith He whose fire in Zion's laid,
   His furnace in Jerusalem!

For sure as He the word hath spoke,
   By Him great Babylon shall fall;
Earth be delivered from her yoke,
   And she be found no more at all.

* Rev. xix. 11—13, 16.   † Isa. xxxi. 4.   ‡ Isa. xxxi. 9.

Then shall you see and know My power,
 When I her burdens shall remove;
On all the earth My spirit shower,
 And fill My Church with light and love!

On high the *windows* opened there,*
 Pour floods of *light*, her heavens quake;
All her bright *orbs* in darkness are,
 And earth's foundations greatly shake.

Her state shall now be broken down;
 Yea, clean dissolved and be no more;
Now to the righteous rest is known,
 With highest praise on ev'ry shore.

BABYLON'S CERTAIN FALL!
Isa. xiv. 4, 5, 22—28.   Rev. xiv. 6—8.   L. M.

102. O Babylon, thy mighty name,
 Thy terrible destroying power,
Thy great renown and wide-spread fame
 Shall sink with thee to rise no more.

For God Himself hath spoken this,
 And who shall disannul His word;
His hand against thee lifted is,
 Nor wilt thou stand before the Lord.

THE SPIRITUAL ENSIGN AND GOSPEL TRUMPET!
Isa. xviii. 3.   L. M.

103. When God His ensign lifteth up,
 As seen upon the mountain top,
Behold ye people from afar,
 And muster for the holy war.

Hear ye the trumpet's certain sound,
 And to His standard gather round;
His mandates willingly obey,
 And fight your battles in His day!

---

* Isa. xiii. 9, 14 & xxiv. 17, 20.

Ye need not faint nor be afraid;
For as the Lord Himself hath said
That He will skill and strength supply,
And lead you on to victory.

Your foes, with all their fighting pow'rs,
In their strong battlements and tow'rs,
Shall like old Jericho be found,
And fall before the trumpet's sound.

When its true voice is heard on high,
Calling His chosen warriors nigh,
Your foes in their strongholds will quail,
And all their warlike courage fail.

Nor earthly weapons He supplies
To war against His enemies;
It's only by the Spirit's sword
We war and triumph in the Lord!

ON GOD'S MOUNTAIN, HIS PEOPLE ARE ENRICHED WITH HIS BLESSINGS, TEMPORAL AND SPIRITUAL!

Isa. xxv. 6—8.

104. On the mountain of God
    No darkness is there;
It is scattered abroad,
    And vanished like air.
For all things are seen
    As naked and bare,
What they should have been,
    And what they now are.

His gifts unto man,
    For drink and for food,
Are made very plain,
    And well understood;
Their *uses* are known,
    And fully approved!
Their *abuses* are shown,
    And also removed!

There Providence brings,
 As heaven decrees,
A feast of *fat* things—
 Of wines on the *lees*;*
Wines well purified,
 The richest and best,
Are amply supplied
 For every guest.

There knowledge is found
 And wisdom begins;
True pleasures abound
 And harmony reigns.
The best of all wine
 Is freely bestow'd:
For the feast is divine
 That cometh from God!

Tears are wiped away
 From every face,
In His holy day
 Of truth and of grace.
The *veil* it is gone,
 The darkness is past;
The true *light* hath shone
 That ever will last!

THE RETURN FROM CAPTIVITY OF THE WANDERING OUTCASTS OF ISRAEL.

Isa. xxvii. 13. L. M.

105. When the great trumpet shall be blown,
And God's salvation be made known,
His outcasts, both far off and nigh,
Will then return to the most High!

Their offerings of praise will bring
Unto their Saviour God and King;
And in His temple Him adore,
Who lives and reigns for evermore.

* Wines passing through the *lees*, and in this way *well refined*, their tendency to fermentation is prevented.

THE SURE FOUNDATION!

Isa. xxviii. 16.   Mat. xvi. 15—18.   7's.

106. See the Church built on the rock,
Which the rod of God hath struck;
This her safety does ensure,
Thenceforth and for evermore.

From this rock salvation rolls,
To restore our dying souls;
The one only living rock,
Which the rod of God hath struck!

To His Church elected pure
All His promises are sure:
Strength with her can never fail,
Nor the gates of hell prevail.

Satan he may vent his rage,
With his legions her engage,
War with all their hellish might,
And be vanquished in the fight.

Jesus is this living rock,
Which the rod of God hath struck;
He did thus His Church redeem,
And it now is built on Him!

Her foundation standeth sure,
And on earth she must endure;
Rise to glory in the end,
Unknown ages there to spend.

THE SAINTS' PROTECTION.

Isa. xxxi. 5.   L.M.

107. As parent birds protect their young,
Hovering, watching over them:
So shall the saints' assembled throng
Be guarded in Jerusalem.

God who is over will defend,
  Defending He'll deliver it ;
While round Him flying hosts attend,*
  To make her enemies submit.

Their presence and their mighty dread
  Shall put the troops of hell to flight ;
Like flames the holy watchers spread,
  And nations tremble at the sight.

Thus shall He do and thus prevail,
  Let Zion's friends and people hear ;
Their means of help can never fail
  With an Almighty helper near !

THE ENSIGN !

Isa. xxxi. 9.

108. Behold the ensign of the Lord,
  A lion strong in might ;
Whose voice in thunder shall be heard
  When He goes forth to fight !

As a fierce lion will dismay,†
  And trample down his foes,
So victory will mark the way
  The kingly warrior goes !

He'll drink of the refreshing stream,
  To aid Him in the fight ;
Earth's warlike heroes meeting Him,
  Will quail before His might.

The trumpet's call is heard afar,
  And lo ! the beast appears ;
His host he musters for the war,
  Amid foreboding fears.

* Dan. iv. 17.   † Isa. xxxi. 4 ; Jer. xxv. 30–33.

When God's great day of wrath is come,*
   All who shall Him withstand,
His jealousy will them consume
   With a destroying hand.

He'll wound the heads o'er many lands;
   Their mighty ones shall fall,
Till men submit to His commands,
   And own Him Lord of all!

"HIS PRINCES SHALL BE AFRAID OF THE ENSIGN!"

Isa. xxxi. 9.   C.M.

109. Behold the ensign of the Lord,
   A lion of great might;
He will His fearful acts record,
   When He goes forth to fight.

For He will roar in going forth,†
   Or like an hero shout,
From east to west, from south to north,
   And all the world throughout.

His voice He utters from on high,
   Which will His foes affright;
And people, both far off and nigh,
   Acknowledge His great might.

They of the ensign are afraid,
   Which from afar is seen;
And fearful voices make them dread
   The battle to begin.

Babylon's stately ruler see
   Into his stronghold pass;
He fears the rumour and doth flee
   Into his hiding-place.

*Psa. cx. 5—7; Rev. vi. 15—17. † Isa. xxxi. 4; Jer. xxv. 30—33.

His princes see the ensign now,
    And are of it afraid ;
They either in submission bow,
    Or fly from it with dread.

See in advance His standard first,
    Lion of awful name ;
He at the brook will slake His thirst,*
    T" sustain His warlike fame !

Just as the eagles' eyes do glance
    Upon the distant prey :
Against His foes He will advance,
    And fill them with dismay.

In Armageddon is the place †
    Where all their armies meet,
Who either flee before His face,
    Or fall beneath His feet.

All who shall dare meet Him in fight
    Will tremble at His word,
Be scattered by His warlike might,
    Or slaughter'd by His sword !

Sinners in Zion are afraid
    Of wrath sounded to them,
Saith He whose fire in Zion's laid,
    Now in Jerusalem.

Then all the earth shall serve the Lord,
    Knowing what He hath done ;
Shall all His righteous acts record,
    And worship Him alone.

GOD'S MESSENGERS.
Isa. lii. 7.
L. M.

110. How beautiful and glorious
    Are those whose willing feet have trod,
And brought their messages to us,
    Upon the mountains of our God.

* Psa. cx. 5—7.   † Rev. xvi. 16.

They in the Master's cause employ
   Their gifts the way of life to teach,
And with a calm and holy joy
   The Gospel of salvation preach.

For the good tidings each one brings,
   And publisheth through Jesus' grace
His dispensation of good things,
   And maketh known the way of peace!

For by their ministry divine,
   The knowledge of our God is giv'n;
As burning, guiding lights they shine,
   And preach and point the way to heav'n.

THE WATCHMEN OF ZION!

Isa. lii. 8—10.   C. M.

111. The watchmen shall lift up their voice,
   Together shall they sing,
And in true fellowship rejoice,
   To praise their God and King.

For they will then see eye to eye,
   And join with one accord,
With light and wisdom to supply
   The churches of the Lord.

For Christ will reign in Zion then,
   And send His servants forth:
With whom His glory will be seen,
   And known throughout the earth.

Both old and young will know the Lord,
   His grace and goodness prove;
And with united voice record
   The praises of His love.

JESUS THE SUCCORER OF TEMPTED AND SORROWFUL SOULS.

Isa. liii. 4, 5 & lxiii. 9.   S. M.

112. Jesus, with glory crowned,
   Who sits enthroned above;
In goodness and in grace renowned,
   And marvellous in love!

   His name true music bears
   To souls oppressed with grief;
He wipes away their flowing tears,
   And brings them sure relief.

   Their troubles may be great,
   But His were greater still;
In pray'rs and tears and bloody sweat,
   Yet resigned was His will!

   And now how great His care
   Their sorrows to remove,
Who in their trouble seek to share
   An int'rest in His love.

   When sore oppressed with fears
   The burdened soul is found,
The music of His name it hears,
   And life is in the sound.

   If tempest-tossed and tried,
   Or suffering from pain,
The promise of His love applied
   Will cheer the soul again.

   In Jesus' name is found,
   As each believer knows,
A healing balm for ev'ry wound,
   And solace for his woes.

THE AFFLICTED AND DESOLATE CONDITION OF GOD'S CHURCH OR PEOPLE.

Isa. liv. 1, &c.   C. M.

113. Mount Zion may be desolate,
    And naked all around;
God's people mourn her fallen state,
    And sit upon the ground.

Her battlements be broken down,
    Her covering removed;
Yet still the Lord has always known,
    And His own people loved!

The nations may dispise her now,
    And treat her with disdain;
For she is fallen very low,
    Yet she shall rise again.

For her redeemer He will come
    To raise her fallen state,
To bring His chosen people home,
    And be their wall and gate.*

When He shall be her wall of fire,†
    And the glory within,
No enemy who may desire
    Shall ever there be seen.

No more His people will be sad
    When Zion is restor'd;
But then His river will make glad ‡
    The city of the Lord!

GOD'S INVITATION.

Isa. lv. 1—3.   C. M.

114. Ho, ev'ry one that thirsteth come,
    The living waters try;
And he that hath *no money* come
    Unto the Lord and buy!

* Psa. cxviii. 20.   † Zech. ii. 5.   ‡ Psa. xlvi. 4.

Through Jesus, the one sacrifice,
  Take bread and water free;
Without *money* and without *price*,
  Buy *wine* and *milk* of Me!

Wherefore do ye your money spend
  For that which is not good,
When I am your Almighty friend,
  And furnish living food?

" Incline your ear, come unto Me,
  Hear and your soul shall live!"
For I your living bread will be,
  And living water give!

A covenant I then will make—
  An everlasting one!
That I no more will you forsake
  Who trust in Me alone.

For the sure mercies of the Lord
  To David shall be yours;
Who trusted in My saving Word
  With all His ransomed pow'rs.

THE FALSE AND THE TRUE FAST!

Isa. lviii. 1—8. 8's & 7's.

115. Is this th' fast that I have chosen?
  Saith the high and mighty God;
While to good your hearts are frozen,
  And forbidden paths are trod.

Is it that you should go drooping
  As a bulrush for a day?
Or to forms of sorrow stooping,
  In your own appointed way?

Do you think it is abstaining
  From such food as others eat?
Or in formal pray'rs remaining,
  In the cloister or retreat?

Is not this what I have spoken,
  To let the oppress'd go free?
That the bands of sin be broken,
  And the bars to liberty?

Is it not to clothe the naked,
  Th' poor and destitute to feed?
And that help should be imparted
  In each case of real need?

Then your light should rise in darkness,
  Clear and bright as the noonday;
And my glory be your riches,
  That will never fade away.

ZION RESTOR'D: OR, THE CHURCH OF GOD GLORIFIED!

Isa. lx. 1, &c.   Psa. lxxxvii. 3.   C.M.

116. The holy city of our God,
  The tabernacles where
He hath prepared His own abode,
  And ever dwelleth there.

Within He is her glorious light,
  Without her wall of flame;
Nations shall tremble at the sight,
  And bow before His name.

In her the living waters flow
  Out from the living throne;
Those waters which His people know,
  And He can give alone.

Those waters like a river pure,*
   Or like a swelling stream,
Swelling and rising more and more,
   Proceedeth forth from Him.

The streams which from that river fall,
   And spread themselves abroad,
Supplieth and rejoiceth all,
   The city of our God!

From Zion songs of holy mirth
   Re-echo everywhere;
She is the praise of all the earth,
   Emmanuel is there!†

GOD'S CHURCH GLORIFIED!
Isa. lx. 1—3.

117. Darkness covereth the earth,
   Gross darkness is on mankind,
Yet on those of heav'nly birth,
   God's elect, His light hath shin'd.

Blissful light is ris'n on them,
   And His glory there is seen,
To enlighten and redeem
   Her that hath afflicted been.

Gentiles hasten to her light,
   Kings to her bright rising speed.
From the regions of the night,
   And the churches of the dead.

All her officers are peace, ‡
   Her exacters righteousness;
Messengers of truth and grace,
   Who with joy and gladness bless.

* Eze. xlvii. 1—5; Rev. xxii. 1.   † Eze. xlviii. 35.
‡ Isa. lx. 17.

She shall hearken to His calls,
    Who in love did her upraise;
His salvation is her walls,*
    And her gates shall be His praise!

Hence her sun shall never set, †
    Never more her light go down;
God will make His Church complete,
    And with all His glory crown!

CHRIST'S POWER IN SAVING HIS CHURCH AND DESTROYING HER ENEMIES.

Isa. lxiii. 1—9.   7's & 6's.

118. Who is this from Edom comes,
    Along the Bozrah road?
Warlike terror He assumes,
    His garments dyed with blood.

I that speak in righteousness,
    Who mighty am to save;
I will now my foes distress,
    And I all power have.

Why is thine apparel red
    Those stains thy garments show,
Like one that does th' winepress tread,
    When grapes with juices flow?

Th' winepress I have trod alone,
    And there were none with me;
Though my friends from me are gone,
    I will their Saviour be!

Now my anger shall be shown,
    And fury me sustain;
I will tread the people down,
    And trample on the slain.

* Isa. lx. 18.   † Ibid. 20, 21.

Now the day of wrath exprest,
  And long foretold is come;
Th' year to give my chosen rest,
  And their oppressors doom.

Now my people here below
  Shall from all yokes be free;
They shall my salvation know,
  My power and glory see!

I will their deliv'rer be,
  To them my mercy prove;
They shall find their all in me,
  And dwell in heav'nly love.

"WE ALL DO FADE AS A LEAF."

Isa. lxiv. 6.

119. Just as the leaf fadeth away,
  When fallen to the ground,
So mortals wither and decay,
  Nor is distinction found.

We like the falling leaf must die,
  And like to it become;
Yea, in one place together lie,
  And dust be made our home.

Nor can we tell how very soon
  This may our portion be:
The season swiftly hastens on
  Which holds our destiny.

The sap of life will soon dry up,
  And then our tott'ring clay
Is like a house without a prop,
  Ready to fall away.

The bases fail, the building falls,
    And all in ruin lies :
Thus perishes our shattered walls,
    When man, the creature dies.

Then what is worldly pomp and power,
    Or beauty, or what else ?
'Tis like the falling of a shower,*
    That the earth soon conceals.

O, then, may we our wisdom prove,
    And show a higher care,
By living for the world above,
    And seek a portion there.

"HEARKEN TO THE SOUND OF THE TRUMPET!"

Jer. vi. 17 ; Zech. ix. 14.   C. M.

120. Hark, from on high the trumpet sounds,
    Inviting souls to rise,
Where everlasting joy abounds,
    And glory never dies !

Ho, all ye needy sinners, hear ;
    The call is sent to you ;
See God himself the witness bear,
    See Christ the tokens show !

Flee from the din of earthly strife,
    Nor make the least delay
To walk the road that leads to life,
    The clear and shining way.

Now, while the trumpet speaks of peace,
    Rise and obey the call ;
Now is the time, the day of grace,
    While peace and pardon fall.

---

* Jas iv. 14 ; 2 Sam. xiv. 14.

Behold, now is salvation nigh,
    The Saviour waiting stands:
He points the road to joys on high,
    And life is in His hands!

This is the way, and this alone,
    In which we must be found,
To meet around the heav'nly throne,
    And tread the hallowed ground.

THE BALM OF GILEAD!

Jer. viii. 22.

121. Is there no balm in Gilead?
    And is there no Physician there?
Of whom advice and help is had,
    If we submit unto his care.

Yes, there is balm in Gilead still,
    Famed for its many wondrous cures!
And a Physician, vast in skill,
    Whose love and pity still endures!

If it be so, why is it thus
    With medicine and help at hand,
Why is that help unknown to us,
    Who seem to dwell in Israel's land?

Alas! the answer is too plain,
    Why we are still so sickly found,
Why we in this weak state remain,
    While enemies enclose us round.

If we sit still and silence keep,
    We in unguarded places are;
And if we watch, and pray, and weep,
    We trust in Egypt's shadow there.

Lord, turn us, and we shall be turn'd.
    Although Thy counsel we forsook,
When we have rightly of Thee learn'd,
    Then we shall only to Thee look.

Then shall we into cities go,
    By truth well fenced and made secure ;
Believe, obey, and worship too,
    Where our protection will be sure.

Th' balm of Gilead shall we know,
    And find the true Physician there,
Who will His healing pow'r bestow,
    And safely keep beneath His care.

THE BALM OF GILEAD!

Jer. viii. 22.

122. The true balm of Gilead is grace,
    The Physician is Jesus alone,
Anywhere is the recognised place,
    That His wonderful cures are all done.

With this medicine always at hand,
    And with such a Physician also,
There is none that within His light stand,*
    That will have long unheeded to go.

Before Him we devoutly appear,
    We keep *silence*, we *watch*, and we pray ;†
The Physician our cases will hear,
    Nor will send us uncared for away.

An infallible remedy, grace,
    Our Physician infallible too ;
His free service then let us embrace,
    And He will a free healing bestow !

* John i. 1—9 ; Heb. iv., 12, 13.   † Isa. xli. 1.

"THE KING OF ETERNITY!"*

Jer. x. 10.   C.M.

123. Jehovah He alone is God,
    The God of life and power;
His throne eternal ages stood,
    And ever shall endure.

Thousands of worlds may pass away,
    Yet He from whom they came,
Continueth now as yesterday,
    And evermore the same.

No lapse of ages can decrease,
    Nor change those years of His;
He now is God, and cannot cease
    To be what now He is.

He reigns all ages who reigns now,
    Though thrones and worlds may fall;
Eternity itself must bow,
    And crown Him Lord of all.

THE WICKEDNESS AND DECEITFULNESS OF THE HUMAN HEART.

Jer. xvii. 9, 10.   L.M.

124 Vile and deceitful is man's heart,
    It's wickedness is very great;
And with it Satan plays his part,
    That he may there maintain his seat.†

Its secret evils who can know?
    Or who it's miseries declare?
God, He alone can fully show,
    The evils that inhabit there.

---

* See margin, Psa. xlvii. 2, 3.   † 1 John v. 19.

For He Himself searches the heart,
   And tries the reins of ev'ry one,
That He may just rewards impart,
   According to the actions done.

Oh may His all-preventing grace
   Redeem and save us from all ill:
That we may seek with joy His face,*
   And learn the pleasures of His will.

GOD'S WORD LIKE A FIRE!

Jer. xxiii. 29.   S. M.

125. God's Word's a living fire,
   A pure immortal flame:
The source of ev'ry good desire,
   Or actions worth the name.

O may He dwell in me,
   And govern all my ways,
That I to Him may faithful be,
   And serve Him all my days!

GOD'S WORD IS LIKE A HAMMER!

Jer. xxiii. 29.   S.M.

126. Just like a hammer He,
   When by its sudden stroke,
However hard the rock may be,
   Is into pieces broke.

Just so He breaks His foes,
   Or melts them with His love;
Thus the same hand that overthrows,
   May their salvation prove!

* Psa. xxvii. 8.

THE RESURRECTION OF DRY BONES!
Eze. xxxvii. 1—14.   L.M.

127. Come from the winds, reviving breath,
    Breathe on these slain that they may live:
Raise them up from their graves of death,
    The promised resurrection give!

These bones are scattered o'er their graves,
    And dry throughout the vale appear;
Come from the winds, O breath that saves
    From guilt, and darkness, and despair!

From the four winds of heav'n above,
    Breathe on these dry and scattered bones:
That they may to each other move,
    And form and shape to skeletons.

Let sinews then and flesh arise,
    And skin cover the whole around;
While wisdom symmetry supplies,
    Till they in perfect forms are found!

Come from the winds, O breath divine,
    Breathe on these forms that they may live:
Reanimate these works of Thine,
    Both light, and life, and spirit give!

So shall the house of Israel rise,
    An army of the living God;
Know and fulfil the prophecies,
    And spread salvation all abroad!

NEBUCHADNEZZAR'S DREAM OF THE GREAT SYMBOLIC IMAGE!
Dan. ii. 31—35.   L.M.

128. Behold the *image* of the King's,
    As seen in visions of the night;
His *form* and *visage* terror flings,
    Before the dreamer's second sight!

His massive head is like fine gold :
  His breast and arms like silver are ;
His belly and his thighs unfold,
  And they with polish'd brass compare.

His legs like iron pillars stand,
  His feet and toes as iron and clay ;
Their *antitypes* the world command,
  And subject all things to their sway !

In him four monarchies appear,
  Their order strength and worth are seen :
The image doth *true symbols* wear
  Of all that governments have been !

His downcast looks plainly portend,
  Marking his feet of iron and clay,
That soon those governments will end,
  Yea, very quickly pass away.

The *stone* will smite the image there,
  Till like the dust the winds engage,
All's swept and lost ; He'll then declare
  His reign through the *millennial age!*

HIEROGLYPHICAL REPRESENTATIONS OF THE FOUR GREAT MONARCHIES OF THE WORLD !

Dan. vii. 1—7. L. M.

129. The lion beast with eagle's wings
  Portrays the greatest earthly kings ;
  This beast did plainly typify
  The Babylonian monarchy.

  The second beast, from the rough sea,
  Is noted for its cruelty ;
  A savage bear, with dreadful paws,
  And very strong devouring jaws.

The government described by this,
The Medo-Persian kingdom is;
And this was very plainly shown,
When Babylon's was overthrown!

As we look to the sea again,
One with *four heads* comes from the main:
A leopard this, it hath *four wings,*
Which it to *speedy* conquests brings!

The Grecian kingdom thus portray'd,
A very wide dominion had;
And the four heads with one rule past,
Show'd its *division* at the last!

The sea in a tempestuous storm,
When a strange beast of dreadful form,
With warlike fury issued forth;
This beast destroyeth all the earth!

As vengeance in the distance loomed,
This monarchy is also doomed!
At its full time we may depend,
This too will have a final end.

When this last change on earth has come,
One will the government assume;*
And His dominion will endure,
Till time shall end and be no more!

THE LITTLE HORN!

Dan. vii. viii., 20—26.   C.M.

130. Behold ten horns upon the beast,
    They represent ten kings!
And then one more which seemed the least,
    After the other springs.

* Dan. vii. 13, 14.

This last, which looks so very small,
    So dwarf'd to human view ;
Puts forth a power to subdue all,
    And ruleth not a few !

He covets kingdoms here below,
    Speaks proudly of great things ;
And all he can, both high and low,
    Into subjection brings.

He worketh wonders in the sight
    Of his own worshippers ;
Claims for his messengers sole right,
    As his interpreters !

For twelve hundred and sixty days,
    Or just so many years ;
He here a double sceptre sways,
    And then its wane appears !

His earthly sun no longer shines,
    For clouds o'ercast his skies ;
His higher glory then declines,
    It fades away and dies.

THE LITTLE HORN !

Dan. vii. viii., 20—22.   7's & 6's.

131. See ten horns, which mean ten kings,
    Upon the reigning beast ;
After them another springs,
    And he appears the least.

He a lesser form contracts,
    And yet more stout is he,
In his words, and in his acts,
    Than any one we see !

With a knowledge of mankind,
    And a perception keen,
He a double claim enjoin'd,
    And hath successful been !

With a rule both far and nigh,
  He utters words of pride :
Both against the Lord most High,
  And all His saints beside.

As by him new laws are made,
  His fame hath widely spread ;
While he carries on a trade
  With living and with dead !

Lo ! he wars against the good,
  Who will not him obey ;
And hath shed innocent blood,
  Where he had pow'r to slay.

But the judgment soon will sit,
  That takes away his power ;
The world will then forsake it,
  And never own it more.

THE LITTLE HORN !

Dan. vii. 20—22.   S. M.

132. Behold the little horn,
    Of anti-christian birth ;
  Professing to be heaven-born,
    Yet cometh from the earth !*

  He claims a pow'r divine,
    A secular also ;
  And therefore always doth incline
    To exercise the two !

  He hath sharp piercing eyes,
    His mouth speaketh great things :
  In subtle words and blasphemies,
    Against the King of kings.

* Rev. xiii. 11.

He weareth out the saints,
  By persecuting laws :
Regardless of their just complaints,
  All pity he withdraws.

He loveth pomp and show,
  And by low arts and wiles,
His worldly treasures overflow ;
  Thus he the weak beguiles !

Yet soon his end shall come,
  And this unrighteous power
The Lord in judgment will consume,
  Till it be known no more.

PETITION.

Dan. vii. 18, 27.   4-6's & 2-8's.

133. Lord of the worlds of light,
  Dwelling in glory bright,
Which mortal man cannot behold ;
  Where is Thy ancient fame,
  The terrors of Thy name,
Of which Thy faithful servants told ?

Oh would'st Thou now awake,
  Thine arm quite naked make,
To get Thy mournful Church renown ;
  Lift up her fallen state,
  Her beauties new create,
And with immortal honors crown.

For when Thou shalt her raise,
  She then shall be a praise,
As all the earth shall see and know ;
  False systems of the world,
  To darkness shall be hurl'd,
And saints reign over all below !

THE LONG-SUFFERING OF GOD!

Hosea xi. 8, 9; 2 Pet. iii. 9, 15.   L. M.

134. How shall I give thee up, saith God?
 Or how shall I deliver thee?
How shall I leave thee in thy blood?
 Or how in mercy set thee free?

How shall I make thee desolate
 By a perpetual barrenness?
How leave thee in thy fallen state,
 And curse thee from thy dwelling-place?

My heart is troubled by the thought,
 And my repentings kindled are,
My Son each captive soul hath bought,
 And I will yet in mercy spare.

I will not yet my wrath employ,
 Their lasting ruin to complete;
I will not totally destroy,
 But spare a little longer yet.

For I am God, and not a man,
 That I should instantly repay;
For I can still devise a plan,
 To turn my gath'ring wrath away.

I can be merciful and just,
 Therefore I will forbearance show;
But should they not repent, they must
 Then meet a final overthrow.

My mercy I to them afford,
 To save them from the coming storm;
But if they will provoke the sword,
 Strict justice shall the work perform.

THE FALSE AND TRUE REST!

Micah ii. 10; Mat. xi. 28—30.   s. m.

135. Arise ye, and depart,
    For this is not your rest;
No outward forms or schools of art
    Will profit in the least.

    No ceremonies plann'd
    By art or man's device,
True rest or quiet can command,
    Nor for its loss suffice!

    No costly off'rings brought,
    With outward pomp and show,
By which the worshippers have sought
    The secret good to know,

    Have ever yet avail'd,
    Or met with a success,
But all their schemes and efforts fail'd
    The blessing to possess!

    As sinners all must learn
    What God's own prophets say:
To know, repent of sin, and turn
    From ev'ry evil way.

    Through faith in Christ alone,
    The faith that works by love,
Rest sought in Him, the holy One,
    Will most successful prove!

THE BREAKER!

Micah ii. 13.   s. m.

136. The breaker, He is come,
    Whose mighty graces move
Our wrathful hardness to consume,
    Or melt it down to love!

He breaks the hardest heart,
  Just like the stricken rock
Before man's Vulcan-strength will part,
  When He the blow hath struck.

He breaks the pow'r of sin
  By a continual stroke,
Till all its hardness felt within
  He hath entirely broke.

He melts the hearts of steel,
  Just like a melting fire,
Until the hardest hearts shall feel
  Their hardness all expire !

Like a refiner's fire
  Will gold and silver try,
Just so His flaming love desire
  Their hearts will purify !

Just like a fuller's soap
  Will purge out ev'ry stain,
He'll work His cleansing process up,
  Till He pure whiteness gain !

He breaketh by His power,
  He smites that He may heal,
That He may by His grace restore,
  And all His love reveal.

He melteth by His love,
  He purifies by grace,
All sin and darkness to remove,
  And show His smiling face !

THE BREAKER !

Micah ii. 13.

137. The breaker by His might
  And majesty will move,
In changing darkness into light,
  And wrathfulness to love !

He breaks the Father's wrath,
   By His all-soft'ning flame;
In Him eternal virtue hath
   Her purest, sweetest name!

He breaks the wrathfulness
   In all created things;
From Him they life and joy possess,
   And shining glory springs!

(The Father worketh by,
   And is honor'd in th' Son;
As He was from eternity,
   Ere this world had begun.)

He breaks the widespread wrath,
   Which sin alone hath made,
By which mankind were plung'd in death,
   When God was disobeyed.

He shed His precious blood,
   To help man in the fall;
And those He reconciles to God,
   To them restoreth all!

THE BREAKER!

Micah ii. 13.   7's & 6's.

138. The breaker manifested hath
   His vast transforming pow'rs;
He who breaks His Father's wrath,
   And who subdueth ours.

He who breaks the hardest wrath,
   And these hard hearts of ours,
Who, as man's Redeemer, hath
   All grace and saving pow'rs!

He who breaks the pow'r of sin,
   Man's great and deadly foe,
When He brings His virtue in,
   To rescue him from woe.

He who breaks the serpent's head,
    When he would tyrant be;
Who doth upon his pow'r tread,
    And set his captives free!

As a mighty breaker does
    His enemies condemn,
So He breaketh all His foes,
    Or else subdueth them.

As a breaker He is great,
    In wrath as well as love;
And He fills the highest seat
    Of all the thrones above!

All that know this breaker's name,
    And by it now saved are,
Will rejoice to sound His fame,
    And praise Him ev'rywhere.

THE BREAKER!

Micah ii. 13.   C. M.

139. He breaks the great red Dragon's power,*
    Who doth all nations lead;
He makes the ruling Beast to cower,
    And filleth him with dread.

He breaks the judges of the land,
    As with an iron rod,
When they in evil judgment stand
    Against a righteous God.

He breaks the potsherds of the earth,
    That dash against His might;
They dare the wrath He sendeth forth,
    And fall beneath its weight.

* Rev. xii. 3; xx. 2; Isa. xxvii. 1.

He breaks the pow'r of wicked men,
  Who persecute the good;
His wrath hath manifested been,
  T' avenge His servants' blood.

He breaks the pow'r in all his foes,
  Of stern, rebellious hand;
Over all such His judgment goes,
  Nor can they it withstand.

All enemies to Him will cower,
  Before His work is done;
His pow'r will subject ev'ry power,
  As He must reign alone!

THE CESSATION OF ALL WAR THE FRUIT OF GOD'S SPIRITUAL TEACHING!

Micah iv. 1—4.   L. M.

140. When from their hills and mountains too,
All people are disposed to go *
Up to the mountain of the Lord,
As taught and guided by His Word:

To hear what He in spirit says,
And learn to walk in all His ways,
All wars and fightings then will cease,
And works of righteousness increase.

The wealth of nations will be great
When men their swords to ploughshares beat,
And warlike instruments are made
To useful implements in trade!

Earth will her choicest blessings give,
And men in peace and plenty live;
The nations will be joined as one,
To fear and serve the Lord alone!

* Jer. iii. 23.

WHAT GOD REVEALS AND WHAT HE REQUIRES.
Micah vi. 8.   4-6's & 2 8's.

141. God unto men hath shown
    What things are good and right,
And He hath made this known
    By His revealing *light*:
By grace they have enlightened been,
And by it *good* and *evil* seen!

    Then what He doth require,
        He may most justly claim,
    As they all good desire
        And mercy seek of Him;
    That His commands they should approve,
    And walk with Him in humble love!

LIGHT AND GRACE FROM GOD.
Micah vi. 8.   L. M.

142. God by His *light* hath plainly show'd, *
    And men have clearly understood,
By knowledge, which He hath bestow'd,
    What is *evil* and what is *good!*

For by His *light* is known within
    Both what He hates and what He loves.
As He condemns for ev'ry sin,
    And ev'ry act that's good approves!

For whatsoever is reprov'd †
    Is manifested by the *light,*
And thoughts, and words, and actions prov'd
    That are accepted in His sight.

God giveth unto men desire,
    And doth on them His grace bestow:
He also doth of them require
    That they the fruits of grace should show.

* Rom. i. 19; John iii. 19—21.   † Ephe. v. 13.

The *pound* is given to man for use— *
    The *talents* that he may improve—
But if those gifts he should abuse,
    They will his condemnation prove.

Be upright and love mercy too,
    This He requires of ev'ry one,
To walk humbly with God also,
    And serve and worship Him alone.

JONAH AND NINEVEH.
See his Book.

143. Jonah, a prophet sent by the Lord
    To preach at old Nineveh, fled,
And madly resisting His word,
    He journeyed for Tarshish instead.

He had found and entered a ship,
    That he from God's presence might flee,
And soon was he seen fast asleep,
    While a storm was lashing the sea!

And when he was fairly awake,
    The mariners hearing his plea,
He counsell'd if but for their sake,
    They should cast him into the sea.

There a fish the Lord had prepar'd,
    Which swallowed the prophet alive;
Then his prayer and vows they were heard,
    And he did the *ordeal* survive!

For th' fish, by command of the Lord,
    Now vomited him on the strand.
Thus Jonah, restor'd by His word,
    Went forth to fulfil His command!

He prophesied Nineveh's fall,
    His fear and its shame he outbraved,
The message was sounded to all,
    And repenting, the city was saved;

* Luke xix. 12—27; Mat. xxv. 14—30.

For many years judgment was stayed,
    Till sin and rebellion had grown,
Then vengeance no longer delayed,
    But Nineveh was overthrown.

NINEVEH'S DESPOTIC RULERS.
Nahum ii. 11—13.   L. M.

144. The lion gloating o'er his prey,
And his young lions, where are they?
Which with their Sire fierce prowlings made,
And none on earth made them afraid.

The lion's roar put men in fear, *
For he would th' prey in pieces tear,
That by his all rapacious greed
He might his lionesses feed!

His holes with heaps of prey he fill'd,
His dens did stores of ravin yield,
That they might have their feast of blood,
And satiate their lust of food!

But where is the old lion now?
He and his lions are laid low;
His lionesses, with their lust,
Have long been buried in the dust.

Earth's rulers may see in this glass
How soon away their glories pass,
When death shall bring its day of gloom,
And justice fix th' oppressor's doom.

If hardened despots in their day
With cruel acts the sceptre sway,
Judgment from His tribunal speeds,
Who a'vengeth all unrighteous deeds.

* Isa. v. 29; Jer. iv. 7; Pro. xxviii. 15, 16, (Men in the nature of Lions).

PRAYING FOR PRESERVATION AND A REVIVAL OF GOD'S WORK.

Hab. iii. 2.
S. M.

145. Revive Thy work, O Lord,
In these desponding years,
Employ Thy spirit and Thy Word
In all Thy worshippers.

O let Thy love be shown,
Unveil Thy smiling face,
Between the times make Thyself known,
By works of power and grace.

In wrath let mercy speak
And plead our cause with Thee,
Till Thou the chains of bondage break,
And set the pris'ners free.

Give now Thy people joy
From scenes of deep distress,
The adversary's hope destroy,
And with salvation bless.

Let not the sons of pride,
Who in their malice join
To persecute us and divide,
Accomplish their design.

In sore temptation's hour,
Should our weak courage fail,
Let not the enemy devour,
Nor Satan's arts prevail.

Be Thou our safe defence
'Gainst all his hellish darts;
Our shield be Thy omnipotence,
For thence all fear departs.

If Thou art always nigh,
By a divine support,
Then we by faith shall dwell on high,
Secure from ev'ry hurt.

>May Thy ambassadors
>   Maintain their worthy name;
>Display their power as conquerors,
>   In noted acts of fame.
>
>So shall Thy Gospel here,
>   Which all Thy servants hail,
>Travel successfully the sphere,
>   And finally prevail.

THE DESTRUCTION OF BABEL AND THE ESTABLISHMENT OF THE ONE TRUE RELIGION UPON THE EARTH!

Zeph. iii. 8, 9.   L. M.

146. Since the confounding of men's tongues,
They've wander'd into many wrongs;
And their unlawful lusts have led
To frequent wars and much bloodshed.

Where lust of gain and pow'r prevail,
There just and upright actions fail;
The sin will drive the good away,
And blind ambition bear the sway.

When fellowship and union cease,
The fruits of evil will increase;
As when the tie of friendship breaks,
It some new source of trouble makes.

Thus Babel in confusion keeps,
While her just retribution sleeps;
And yet the time, now hasting fast
Will bring her punishment at last.

The hand of justice will o'ertake
All that the way of truth forsake:
And universal vengeance, then,
Mark the rebellious among men.

Thence unity and concord will
Their kindly influence distil :
And men on righteous acts intent,
Will serve the Lord with one consent.

"UPON ONE STONE SHALL BE SEVEN EYES!"

Zech. iii. 9 and iv. 10.   C. M.

147. The stone, very precious and bright,
    Before the churches laid,
With its eyes of the streaming light,
    A *mystic* meaning had.

Its seven eyes have always been,
    And it has many more,
Which from eternity have seen,
    And will for evermore !

They are the uncreated sight
    Of Christ, the living Lord,
Who is the everlasting light,
    And the *all-seeing* Word !*

They are the *seven lamps* of fire, †
    Before the throne of God :
Which no replenishing require,
    To stream their light abroad.

For they the *seven spirits* are, ‡
    And these, we understand,
Are operating ev'rywhere,
    In one eternal band !

And so this mysterious stone
    Is the creative power,
For He is the Almighty One,
    Who liveth evermore.

* Heb. iv. 12—14.   † Rev. iv. 5.   ‡ Rev. v. 6.

PRISONERS OF HOPE!
Zech. ix. 12.

148. Turn you to the strong hold,
    Ye prisoners of hope;
Encouragements for you unfold,
    And help you to look up.

See in the living Rock,
    Shelter from storm and wind,*
Where all the tribulated flock,
    A place of safety find!

Dangers may them surround,
    And Satan ply his arts,
Yet perfect safety there is found,
    From all his hellish darts.

Whatever blasts may fall,
    Whatever storms may rise,
They are secure amidst them all,
    Nor know a dread surprise.

Ye forlorn of our race,
    Who still in darkness grope,
Seek ye the strong hold of this place,
    As prisoners of hope!

Both faith and hope revive,
    As in this *rock* you rest;
And God will say unto you, Live,
    And be for ever blest.

THE SWORD OF DIVINE JUSTICE SMITING THE INNOCENT TO SAVE THE GUILTY!
Zech. xiii. 7.   Mat. xxvi. 31.

149. Against my fellow, saith the Lord,
Must justice now awake my Sword!
Against my Shepherd, sword, awake,
Of Him a sacrifice to make!

* Isa. xxv. 4.

Stern justice, with its wrathful breath,
Must smite the Shepherd to His death,
That sinful man, for whom He dies,
May from his fallen state arise!

The Holy One, faithful and true,
Must suffer death—to rebels due:
For sinners He must shed His blood,
To reconcile them unto God!

How great and marvellous His love,
Which did such matchless mercy move,
That rebel men might be forgiv'n,
And with the angels dwell in heav'n!

"THE LORD SHALL BE KING OVER ALL THE EARTH!"

Zech. xiv. 9.* C. M.

150. Rejoice ye righteous in the Lord,†
 And glory in His name;
The praises of His love record,
 And sound abroad His fame.

The honors of Jehovah spread
 In ev'ry distant land:
That so the mighty Maker's dread
 May the whole earth command.

Look forward to that happy day,
 For it will surely come,
When He shall earthly kingdoms sway,
 And their sole rule assume!

When all mankind shall know the Lord,
 And bow before His throne;
His name be fear'd, prais'd, and ador'd,
 And He worshipped alone.

* Psa. xlvii. 2, 3.   † Psa. xxxii. 11. and xxxiii. 1.

PRAISE FOR THE SPIRITUAL MANIFESTATIONS OF GOD IN HIS TEMPLE.

Mal. i. 11; Psa. xxix. 9. 4-6's & 2-8's.

151. Let Britons sound aloud
    The praise of Zion's King,
And to His Temple crowd,
    Their offerings to bring;
For there he doth His name declare,
He manifests His glory there.

    There He proclaims His love,
        And makes His mercy known:
    Yea, from His place above,
        Sends joy and gladness down;
For though He dwells in courts on high,
In presence He is always nigh!

    His omnipresence fills
        Immensity of space,
    And He Himself reveals
        To all that seek His face;
His approbation they enjoy,
And in His praise their tongues employ.

    Then to His temple throng,
        And know Him good and great,
    Raise a triumphal song.
        And strains of praise repeat:
In faith and love which he hath giv'n,
Worship the holy King of heav'n.

GOD IS UNCHANGEABLE.
Mal. iii. 6.

152. Not one thing hath fail'd to me
    Of all the Lord hath spoken,
True unto His word is He,
    And it was never broken.

All his promises are sure
  On the conditions given,
They are fixed for evermore,
  As the pillars of heaven.

God is the Unchangeable,
  And faithful in all He says;
But poor man is mutable,
  And inconstant in his ways.

If he stableness would know,
  To the Lord alone he must
In his sojourn here below
  Seek for strength in Him to trust.

THE BIRTH OF CHRIST.

Mat. i. xxiii.; Isa. vii. 14.

153. Let notes of honor swell
  The glad news of the morn,
When Jesus, our Emmanuel,
  Was of a virgin born.

  Incarnate he appears,
  Veiled in a house of clay,
A servant's form the Saviour wears,
  Did thus Himself array.

He stoops from heav'n to earth,
He lays His glory by,
Becomes a mortal man by birth,
  And condescends to die.

Herein the mighty God
  Appeareth wonderful;
His matchless love and mercy show'd
  In off'ring up His soul!

And by this act, renowned
For its surpassing grace ;
The everlasting Father crowned
Himself the Prince of Peace !

Then may our hearts rejoice,
As we thank-off'rings bring,
And worship with a cheerful voice
Jesus our lowly King.

PEACEMAKERS ARE GOD'S CHILDREN.

Mat. v. 9.   7's & 6's.

154 Blessed are the peacemakers,
For they God's children are ;
Of His grace they're partakers,
And in His mercies share.

Opposed to wars and fighting,
And ev'ry evil thing ;
In works of peace uniting,
They serve their God and King.

He hath pronounc'd them blessed,
His blessing they possess,
Who daily stand confessed,
His living witnesses.

Their good and peaceful labors
The God of peace approves,
Bestows on them His favors,
Whose loving works He loves.

THE JEWISH LAW WITH ITS PASSOVER FUL-
FILLED IN JESUS CHRIST.

Mat. v. 17—20 ; and xxvi. 17—20.   8's & 7's.

155. The yearly feast, the Passover,
Unto all the Jews well known,
Jesus Christ, the Lord and Saviour,
Celebrated with His own.

The legal rights and ceremonies
    Of the old Mosaic law,
And the whole circle of its duties,
    Him their light and glory saw!

As a looking-glass will shadow
    Forms that pass or come before it,
Or a shade its form will borrow
    From the thing reflecting it:

Jesus was the soul and substance,
    All the customs taught the same,
Granted for the Jews' observance,
    Until He their *Shiloh* came!

Like the sun shining above us,
    Giving light to all below,
So His *light*, when shining in us,
    All the things of God will show!

Th' moon its light and glory borrows
    From the sun, its changes prove:
So the moon of Jewish shadows
    From Christ, th' Sun of light and love!

ALMS-GIVING.*
Mat. v. 42.

156. Give to him that asketh thee,
    Open lib'rally thine hand,
Let thy charities be free,
    As the Saviour gives command:

Empty send thou none away,
    By to-morrow I will give,
If thou hast it now to-day,
    Dost thou know that thou shalt live?

Is life certain for an hour?
    Yet we know that death is sure;
Let not pride thine alms devour
    While the needy want endure.

* Alms-giving should not be indiscriminate.

What thy hand findeth to do,
  Do it now with all thy might ;
Do not present times forego,
  Riches soon will take their fligh

If it our affections stole,
  What is all earth's sordid gain
But a leprosy of soul,
  And a source of future pain.

If the needy now partake
  Of our charity below,
Some new friendships thus to make*
  We in Paradise may know.

PRAYER.

Mat. vi. 5—15.

157. Prayer is not discovered in words,
  As most seem inclined to believe,
But in life which th' Spirit affords,
  Whose witness His servants receive.

Long prayers at best are in vain,
  By th' art of man's wisdom prepar'd ;
Like th' heathen who think to obtain,
  Because they say much to be heard.

God knoweth the things that we need,
  Before we can speak them to Him,
And He will bestow them indeed,
  In His own good pleasure and time.

By th' Spirit we ask and receive,
  By th' Spirit we seek and we find,
By th' Spirit we knock and believe,
  Who giveth His *light* in the mind.

All this may be inwardly known,
  When words cannot utter our wants,
The Spirit within us may groan,
  Who oft intercedes for the saints.

* Luke xvi. 9.

In the closet we enter to pray
    To our Father in secret there,
Who knows what we inwardly say,
    And His rewards openly are.

But should He dispose us to speak
    By th' help which His Spirit affords :
We then from pure silence may break,
    And utter our wants, too, in words.

Thus th' sacrifice God doth prepare,
    In th' way He Himself doth require,
Our off'rings accepted now are,
    Offered with the true living fire.

PETITION.

Mat. vii. 7, 8.   S's & 7's.

158. God of mercy and salvation,
    We would humbly seek Thy face,
Sensible of acceptation,
    By the Spirit of Thy grace.

We would humbly sue Thy favour,
    In Thine own appointed way ;
Trust in Christ, our only Saviour,
    For the blessing we now pray.

We, as such who say they know Thee,
    Do desire the truth to show :
Serve, adore, and glorify Thee,
    In our trial-state below.

Lord, impart a moral fitness ;
    This, in special mercy give—
That we may by action witness
    To the same, long as we live.

THE BROAD WAY! AND THE NARROW WAY!

Mat. vii. 13, 14; Luke xiii. 24.   C.M.

159. How many thousands walk the road
 That leads to death and hell!
For the enchanting way is broad,
 Where sin's deceptions tell.

The gate is *wide* that leads among
 Those travellers to wrath;
And multitudes into it throng,
 And tread the beaten path.

Directly opposite doth lay
 The road that leads to God:
Strait is the gate, *narrow* the way,
 And oh, how little trod!

But few obey the heav'nly call,
 On the conditions giv'n—
Are willing to forsake their all,*
 And follow Christ to heav'n.

At sacrifice nature recoils,
 And persecution dreads:
For it her int'rest nature spoils,
 And to dishonor leads.

But those that do not enter in
 The strait, the living gate,
Will surely perish in their sin,
 And reap the sinner's fate.

THE GOOD TREE AND THE EVIL TREE.

Mat. vii. 15—20; Luke vi. 43—45.   8's.

160. The tree by its fruit is declar'd,
 Yea, is to a certainty known;
And as this may seem to judge hard,
 The truth shall be presently shown.

* Luke xiv. 33.

Do men gather grapes from the thorns?
　Or can figs from th' thistles be plucked?
So truth a foul evidence scorns,
　However right reason be mocked.

Can the man new born of His God
　Work evil and righteousness too?
Who knows it as his highest good,
　The works of his Saviour to do?

Can the man that liveth in sin,
　Whose affections are woven with earth,
Discover those fruits which sustain
　And infallibly prove the new birth?

The humble, who unto God live,
　Cannot with transgressors take part,
Nor sinners pure evidence give
　That a' change has took place in their heart.

This is the criterion, then,
　By which we may clearly decide
Which are the good trees among men,
　Where only good fruit shall abide.

OBEDIENCE NECESSARY TO ASSURE US OF OUR ACCEPTANCE WITH GOD.

Mat. vii. 21.　　　　L. M.

161. Not ev'ry one that saith Lord, Lord,
　　Will be received of God in heav'n,
　But he that doth obey the Word
　　In all His holy precepts giv'n.

　　Christ doth not choose the hypocrite
　　　For an inheritor of bliss,
　　But him whose inward pow'rs unite
　　　To serve Him with true faithfulness.

Not all that in profession shine,
   Will stand accepted in His sight,
But only they whose hearts incline
   To serve the Lord their God aright.

Such will He at the last receive
   Into the mansions of His love,
For ever with Himself to live
   In glorious happiness above.

THE STORM SPIRITUALIZED!

Mat. viii. 23—27.   S. M.

162. Lord of the winds and waves,
   Us in the storm behold,
See how the mighty tempest raves,
   No helm the ship can hold.

We ready are to sink
   And perish in the sea,
But still on Thy kind presence think,
   And mercy is our plea!

To Thee we cry aloud,
   Who seemest as asleep,
O Lord, disperse the threat'ning cloud,
   And still the raging deep.

The roaring winds control,
   Command them to be still,
Nor let the swelling billows roll,
   Which would the vessel fill.

If Thou shalt speak the word,
   'Tis instantly obeyed:
The waters know their sov'reign Lord,
   And their proud waves are stayed.

In Thee alone we trust,
  And on Thy presence stay,
Nor can our driven bark be lost,
  Nor we be cast away.

We soon shall see a calm,
  The heav'nly *bow* appears,
And off'rings shall Thy name embalm,
  Which saves us from our fears.

ENCOURAGEMENT AND REST FOR THE WEARY.

Mat. xi. 28—30. 7s.

163. Weary sinners go to God,
He will rid you of your load;
He will ease you of your pains;
He will save you from your sins.

Can you doubt His mercy—no;
Surely it cannot be so;
If His promises are sure,
What could sinners wish for more?

For what reason should you doubt?
He in no wise will cast out;
This He solemnly hath said,
Wherefore should you be afraid?

He is pitiful and kind,
And you will acceptance find,
If you do believe His word,
If you trust a faithful Lord.

Cast yourselves, then, at His feet,
Him in Jesus' person meet;
Plead His all-atoning blood
To ensure the peace of God.

If you thus His grace invoke,
Sure as He the word hath spoke,
Pard'ning mercy will be giv'n,
Rest, and happiness, and heav'n.

JESUS THE FRIEND OF SINNERS BOTH BY PRECEPT AND EXAMPLE.

Mat. xxi. 6—9.   8's & 7's.

164. Behold th' meek and lowly Saviour,
    Riding on an ass's colt,
Unassuming His behaviour,
    To all pride a thunderbolt.

He who was the Lord of glory,
    Stooped to shame and poverty,
And through all His mortal story,
    Pure, unfeigned humility!

He who was the Prince of princes,
    Ruling in the worlds of light,
Th' most amazing love evinces
    Unto men in nature's night.

He labored early to instruct them,
    Sought by miracles to move;
Died and rose, thus to redeem them,
    Pleading for their souls above!

In all lands so long benighted,
    Like the dawn of coming day,
All by Jesus' light are lighted, *
    He's their *light*, their *life*, their *way!*

He's the joy of ev'ry nation, †
    The desire of all has come;
He alone is their salvation,
    He whose kingdom is their home.

* John i. 4, 8, 9. and xiv. 6.   † Hag. ii. 7.

AN INSPIRED SONG OF PRAISE TO CHRIST.

Mat. xxi. 9 ; Mark xi. 9, 10. L.M.

165. Hosanna to King David's Son,
    The dual heir of royal blood,
Who sitteth on His Father's throne,
    As Son of man and Son of God!

Hosanna to the heav'nly King!
    Hosanna to the Lord, the Christ!
Who doth for us salvation bring,
    Hosannas to Him in the high'st!

THE REIGN OF TERROR AND ITS PREDICTED END.

Mat. xxiv. 12, 13, 22. S's.

166. Iniquity triumphs and reigns,
    And seems with sad speed to gain ground :
Fast binding its captives in chains,
    And spreading its terrors around.

Yea, wickedness lifts up its head,
    And bears the superior sway,
Filling the whole world with its dread,
    And driving all goodness away.

In manifold forms and degrees,
    Sin a treach'rous influence has,
And Satan his interest sees
    In supporting his own hellish cause.

But shall it for ever be so,
    And th' Lord not His Zion befriend?
Methinks I hear one answer "No!"
    That for her sake it must have an end!

Apollyon shall not govern long,
   Nor his agents their triumphs enjoy,
For vengeance to God doth belong,
   Who will still greater pow'r employ.

For th' time is fast hastening on,
   When truth will His triumphs sustain:
Then all will bow down to the Son,
   And the saints universally reign!

THE LAST JUDGMENT.

Mat. xxv. 31—46.

167. Hark the Judgment trumpet speaks,
    The summons swiftly flies;
Mortality to life awakes,
    The sleeping dead arise.
Thousands, thousands issue forth,
    Upstarting with astonished view,
From the dark places of the earth,
    Which long their silence knew.

See the Judge enthroned descends
    With th' angelic throng,
Greeted by His ransomed friends,
    Whom death hath held so long.
The graves can these no longer keep
    From their home in paradise;
In Jesus' love they fell asleep,
    And by His power they rise!

See th' eternal Judgment set,
    Assembled worlds draw near;
Men and angels all are met,
    Most solemn truths to hear.

Saints will now before Him stand,
　　Clothed in His victorious grace,
But sinners flee at His command,
　　Nor stand before His face.

The day is joyous unto those
　　That rise to dwell in heav'n,
But none their horrors can disclose,
　　Who from their Judge are driv'n.
That hear Him say, Depart ye curs'd
　　To everlasting fire ;
Ye are my foes, and ever must
　　Endure my wrathful ire.

THE BREAD AND WINE USED AT THE PASSOVER SYMBOLIZED THE *SPIRITUAL* BODY AND BLOOD OF CHRIST.

Mat. xxvi. 26—29; John vi. 48—56, 63.　　L. M.

168. When at the yearly Jewish feast,
　　Jesus had taken bread and wine,
He handed them to ev'ry guest,
　　And taught them lessons most divine.

The bread was for a *symbol* giv'n,
　　Of that which does true life afford :
The bread that cometh down from heav'n,
　　The living body of the Lord!

So, when the wine He handed round,
　　He told them *all* to drink of it :
For each one was a sinner found,
　　And so each one had need of it !

For at the Passover it was,
　　And always had a *figure* been,
Of Christ's shed blood, who thereby has
　　Been made a sacrifice for sin.

He is Himself the living bread,
　　The bread and wine but *symbols* are
Of the true bread, and His life shed
　　For man's salvation ev'rywhere!

Thence He no more would drink such wine,
　　As He to His disciples show'd;
But drink with them the new divine,
　　Now in the kingdom of their God.

PETER'S FALL.

Mat. xxvi. 69—75.   C.M.

169. Christians who think they stand secure,
　　And do not watch and pray
That they each trial may endure,
　　Are sure to go astray.

Such should consider Peter's case,
　　Who pledg'd his honest word,
And thought he had sufficient grace,
　　Not to deny his Lord.

All such as on their strength presume,
　　Nor seem, like him, afraid,
Will fail when the temptations come,
　　As Jesus plainly said.

Peter, who follow'd Him afar, *
　　A lesson may afford,
Did soon prevaricate and swear,
　　And thus disown'd his Lord.

Jesus, though not a word He spoke, †
　　Did but one look impart,
One friendly, piercing glance, which broke
　　Poor boasting Peter's heart!

　　* Mat. xxvi. 58.　† Luke xxii. 61, 62.

The fallen one, melted to tears,
  Self-confidence now gone,
A lowly penitent appears,
  To trust in grace alone!

His case a warning is to all,
  To put their trust in God,
Kept by His pow'r they will not fall,
  For such have always stood.

THE SUFFERINGS OF CHRIST.

Mat. xxvii. 26—31 ; Luke xxiii. 27—31, 47, 48.

170. Jesus, who suffered death for men,
  Who bore His cross in shame and pain,
After He mocked and scourged had been
  With proud contempt and sore disdain;

Then He their hour of darkness felt, *
  And the fell pow'r of demons' spite,
Enough the hearts of stone to melt,
  With grief and wonder at the sight.

If those that came together there
  Lamented and bewailed the Lord;
And many conscience-stricken were
  Who the sad tragedy deplor'd:

Well may we in amazement own,
  Reflecting on His suff'rings thus,
The love and pity He hath shown,
  Who suffered, bled, and died for us!

* Luke xxii. 44, 53.

THE RESURRECTION OF JESUS CHRIST.

Mat. xxviii. 1—4.   L. M.

171. Behold the Christ, the Holy One,
    Whose glory struck the watchers dumb,
Roll back and sit upon the stone
    Which barr'd the entrance to His tomb!

Those means His enemies employ'd,
    Lest some His body should remove,
He by His presence rendered void,
    While they His resurrection prove!

As the first streaks of daylight shone,
    When He His sepulchre forsook,
And sat in triumph on their stone,
    Our Mother Earth trembled and shook.

Then He the victory achieved
    O'er sin and death, hell and the grave!
And all that have in Him believed,
    He doth and will for ever save!

THE FEARFUL ENCOURAGED TO EXERCISE FAITH AND TRUST IN GOD.

Mark v. 36.   C. M.

172. Be not afraid, ye doubting souls,
    Believe and trust in God,
Whose mercy as an ocean rolls
    Through the all-pleading blood.

Lo! Christ the Saviour of our race *
    Hath merited for us
Salvation, realized by grace,
    And manifested thus!

* 1 Tim. iv. 10; 1 John ii. 1, 2.

Unbounded as immensity,
  Is His redeeming love!
And lasting as eternity
  Will to His people prove

Thus, they delivered from their fears,
  Though for a season tried,
Will in full answer to their pray'rs
  Have all their wants supplied.

HELL.

Mark ix. 43—48; Isa. lxvi. 24.

173. Alas, my soul, what horror reigns
  In the abodes of black despair;
What fearful darkness, fire, and chains,
  What gloomy, thick, infernal air.

Woes upon woes that never cease
  The wrathful vengeance to fulfil;
Torments on torments that increase,
  Yet are in their commencement still.

When ages have their torments told,
  Still the huge catalogue remains;
And fiery characters unfold
  The endless tenor of their pains.

Eternity alone can tell
  Which hath the dreadful curses framed,
What are the punishments of hell,
  And write the dolors of the damned.

ASKING A PRESENT BLESSING.

Mark xi. 24.

174. Pray we all unto the Lord,
  All unite with one accord,
  Now to supplicate the grace,
  We desire each to embrace.

Would we not salvation have?
Do we not the blessing crave
Christ has promised to bestow?
Why not ask and have it now?

He is able, willing too,
All we ask of Him to do;
Cries, If it you would receive,
Be not faithless, but believe;

Me believe, for I am true,
Trust My word, My promise sue;
I will hear and answer prayer,
And you shall My mercy share.

THE BIRTH OF CHRIST.

Luke ii. 4—20. L. M.

175. Jesus was of a virgin born,
    His messengers the "good news" tell
With pure devotion on the morn
    The Lord appeared with men to dwell.

Angels of light make known His birth,*
    To shepherds the "glad tidings" bring;
"Good will to men" "and peace on earth,"
    "Glory to God," the angels sing!

The shepherds haste to Bethlehem †
    The Saviour's advent to declare;
By a *new star* which shone to them ‡
    The eastern Sages are led there!

The holy babe in manger laid,
    The Magi wondering behold,
As they to Him due homage paid
    With timely offerings and gold.

* Luke. ii. 8—14.   † Luke. ii. 15—20.   ‡ Mat. ii. 1—12.

For He came not as great ones come,
    Who worldly wealth and glory had;
Here He had no abiding home,
    Nor was He in rich garments clad.

Who made and who upholds all things,
    Did shame and poverty endure;
Yea, He who is the King of kings,
    Who lives and reigns for evermore.

THE ADVENT.

Luke ii. 4—20.   S. M.

176. Emmanuel appear'd,
    Poor sinners to redeem;
And many the glad tidings heard,
    And rendered praise to Him.

    An angel came from heav'n
      With the celestial band,
Which then made known a Saviour giv'n
    By the divine command.

    They glory gave to God,
      They proclaim'd peace on earth;
And spread th' glorious news abroad,
    With holy joy and mirth.

    Shepherds, with gladness crown'd,
      To David's city went,
And there the lowly Jesus found,
    The true Messiah "sent!"

    The eastern Sages, led
      By star that shone to them,
With gifts and off'rings worshippéd
    The Lord at Bethlehem.

Come let us now awake
Out of our dreams of earth,
The slumber from our spirits shake
By strains of lowly mirth.

He came on man's account,
And we His love record,
Our good with Him was paramount,
And we will praise the Lord.

THE PENITENT PRAYING FOR PARDON AND PEACE.

Luke v. 31, 32.

177. Physician of the sin-sick soul,
Thy pity I implore :
Let Thy good Spirit make me whole,
And perfect health restore.

Diseased and full of sin I am,
But Thou hast pow'r to heal ;
Now let Thy mercy life proclaim,
And grace my pardon seal.

Deliver me from all my fears,
And calm my troubled breast,
In kind compassion wipe my tears,
And give me peace and rest.

Now let Thy saving mercy flow,
And sin and death remove ;
So shall my happy spirit know
And triumph in Thy love.

JESUS CHRIST HAD NO EARTHLY HOME.

Luke ix. 57, 58.

178. The foxes have holes for their home,
And ev'ry bird flies to its nest ;
The creatures, wherever they roam,
Have places for sleep and for rest.

The Saviour, the Maker of all,
    Renouncing the world from His birth,
Had no certain home where to call,
    In city, or village on earth.

He had nowhere to lay His head
    From wearisome toils of the day:
His want and His poverty lead,
    And point out to all the right way.

The way of true life is above,
    To all who the world would forsake;
Its riches, its honors, its love,
    And Jesus for their pattern take.

THE GOOD SAMARITAN.

Luke x. 30—35.   C. M.

79. Th' man that from Jerusalem went
    Down unto Jericho,
Was wounded, robb'd, fell sick and faint,
    And knew not what to do.

A teaching Priest who saw him lie
    In pain and nakedness,
From sordid motives passed him by,
    And left him in distress.

Likewise a Levite went that way,
    And for a while he stood,
Looked on the man, then turned away,
    And left him in his blood.

But a despised Samaritan,
    Their scorn and their byword,
He had compassion on the man,
    And did true help afford!

He healing remedies applied,
  To ease him of his pain,
And paid for needful help supplied,
  Till he should strength regain.

Thus, while both Priest and Levite taught
  A love in cold pretence,
This stranger into action brought
  Its truthful evidence.

MARTHA AND MARY.
Luke x. 38—42.

180. While Mary sat to hear her Lord,
With others round the cheerful board,
Martha in serving sought her part,
Unwisely cumbered with the art.

With hasty concern she address'd
Her noble and illustrious guest.
Dost thou not care or feel for one
That I am left to serve alone?

Thou, who dost all things understand,
Will sure my sister's help command:
Bid her, therefore, with me to care,
And in this service take her share.

But, Martha, Martha, He returned,
Mary a higher care hath learned;
Her care is just as thine should be,
To hear the truth, and learn of Me.

If thou art troubled and perplexed,
With many earthly trifles vexed,
The part which Mary doth prefer,
Shall not be' taken away from her.

One thing is needful unto thee,
Which will from anxious troubles free,
The holy government of grace,
Where ev'ry duty is in place!

PRAYING FOR SPIRITUAL BLESSINGS.

Luke xi. 13; Mat. vii. 11.   S. M.

181. Pour out Thy spirit, Lord,
    On those assembled here,
And help us all with one accord *
    To seek Thy face in prayer.

    To pray in living faith
    That so we may receive
Those blessings which Thy goodness hath
    And mercy waits to give.

    We know Thou wilt bestow
    The blessings that we need,
If we believe Thy promise now,
    And confidently plead.

    O give the living pow'r,
    The pow'r of faithful prayer,
So shall we know in this glad hour
    How sure Thy mercies are.

THE STRAIT GATE.

Luke xiii. 24.   7's & 6's.

182. The gate of life to enter,
    The soul must seek and strive,
In Christ, its sun and centre,
    Who keepeth it alive.

Without its Lord and Saviour,
    The soul can nothing do;
It's by His strength and favor
    It getteth safely through.

Then wait upon Him fully,
    Yea, look to Him alone,
And trust His power wholly
    By which it will be done.

* Acts ii. 1—4.

In Him thy help is given
    The gate and narrow way,
The only road to heav'n
    And everlasting day.

THE PRODIGAL SON.

Luke xv. 11, &c.   4-6's & 2-8's

183. Behold the prodigal
    Leaving his father's home,
He takes with him his all,
    Far in the world to roam :
Departing from parental cares
To revel in temptation's snares.

He wastes his substance fast,
    He soon hath spent his all,
And bitterly at last
    He sees and feels his fall,
When all his sinful pleasures fail
And want and poverty prevail !

His hunger now is great,
    And in his urgent need
He fain the husks would eat
    On which the swine will feed,
His taskmaster, cruel and hard,
For him nor his sad want has cared.

He now begins to learn
    From sin all troubles come,
And voweth to return
    Unto his Father's home,
Hoping by penitence to move
Compassion from a Father's love !

The Father sees his son
　While yet far off he is,
And earnestly doth run
　To 'mbrace him with a kiss!
The robe and diadem he brings,
Arraying him with costly things!

A feast he doth ordain,
　And music's charms resound,
The dead he lives again
　For the lost son is found!
To him is now salvation come,
Rejoicing in his Father's home!

THE FEAST! C. M.

184. Now let the fatted calf be slain
　　And festive joys abound,
My son was dead, but lives again!
　　Was lost but now is found!

As Father, I ordain a feast,
　I music's charms employ,
And now invite each welcome guest
　To celebrate the joy.

Then sound your harps with magic strain
　And let the news fly round,
My son was dead, but lives again!
　Was lost, but now is found!

DIVES AND LAZARUS.
Luke xvi. 19—31. C. M

185. See Lazarus the beggar laid
　　Before the rich man's gate
To whom honors are daily paid
　　In all the pomp of state.

In gorgeous clothing he appears
    Of costly purple dye,
On viands which his table bears
    He feasts most sumptuously;

While at his gate the beggar lies,
    Desiring to be fed
With wasted crumbs from rich supplies
    His table overspread.

He suffers sorely from disease,
    And his sad case deplores,
While even dogs, to give him ease,
    Would come and lick his sores.

It came to pass the beggar died,
    To whom no help is giv'n,
And Angels as his escort vied,
    To bear his soul to heav'n.

In time the rich man also died,
    And he was buried too
In all the pomp of worldly pride,
    But where did his soul go?

In hell he lifted up his eyes,
    His soul in torments dire,
Where is the worm that never dies *
    And the unquenchèd fire.

From hell he Abraham perceives
    And Lazarus far off,
Lazarus in his bosom lives,
    Though once the rich man's scoff.

He prays—Father Abraham send
    Lazarus to obtain
One drop of water to befriend
    And ease my tongue of pain.

    * Mark ix. 43—48.

But Abraham to him replied,
    Son, thy past life review,
When good things were to thee supplied,
    While Lazarus evil knew.

But now in happiness he lives,
    Has all he can desire,
Thy soul its just reward receives
    The torment of its fire. *

He further prayeth him to send
    Unto his family,
Lest they also in hell should find
    A home of misery.

But Abraham this answer gave—
    That if they will repent,
They Moses and the prophets have,
    And these to them are sent.

If, as the servants of the Lord,
    Their word inspires no dread,
So neither would the warning word
    Of one sent from the dead!

THE PHARISEE.

Luke xviii. 9—14.

186. The Pharisee devoutly prayed,
    As he in God's own temple stood,
Whose trust was on his duties stayed,
    And thought his plea was very good.

For in the week he fasted twice,
    Gave tithes of all he did possess,
Such offerings must sure suffice
    To constitute a righteousness.

* Isa. xxvi. 11.

Nor was he as some others are
  Whose avarice is seen and known,
Who only for self-int'rest care
  And will not their injustice own.

Their moral character was bad,
  They in forbidden paths have trod,
While pious actions made him glad
  And reconciled him unto God.

THE PUBLICAN.
Luke xviii. 9—14.   C.M.

187. The Publican, with grief and shame,
  Confessed his sins to God,
And mercy sought, which freely came
  Through Him it is bestow'd.

He had no righteousness to plead,
  No merits of his own,
But sought for pardon to be freed
  From guilt which weigh'd him down.

His penitential cries were heard
  By Him who dwells in heav'n,
And punishment of sins he fear'd
  Were freely all forgiv'n.

The Pharisee was grace denied
  Who urged a carnal plea;
The Publican was justified,
  Who sought God's mercy free. *

"THE BLIND RECEIVE THEIR SIGHT!" †
Luke xviii. 35—43.   C.M.

188. As Jesus passed near Jericho
  He many follow'rs had,
They saw His pow'rs of healing too, ‡
  And were by Him made glad.

* Luke xviii. 14.   † Mat. xi. 5.   ‡ Luke xix. 37.

A poor blind man, who the same day,
    Sat begging for his bread,
And hearing many pass that way
    With light and hasty tread,

He asked the cause with earnest mood,
    And quick was the reply—
Jesus, a Prophet, great and good,
    He now is passing by!

No sooner had he heard the word,
    Than with an urgent plea
He cried, Thou Son of David, Lord,
    Have mercy now on me!

Some in their zeal unwisely tried
    To make him hold his peace,
But he with more vehemence cried,
    Nor would his pleading cease.

Compassion did the Saviour move
    For one in nature's night
He called him with His call of love,
    And gave him precious sight!

As he in Jesus did believe,
    And wholly trust His word,
With joy he did his sight receive
    And magnify his Lord.

THE MYSTICAL SIGNS!

Luke xxi. 25—28.   7's & 6's.

189. The signs of Jesus' coming
    To judge the Beast and "Whore,"
Are in the distance looming,
    And nearing more and more.

In the sun the *signs* are giv'n,
    And in the moon and stars,
In all the host of heaven,
    But very plain in Mars!

The sea and its waves roaring,
    The wars and tumults great,
Their *mystic signs* are pouring
    Upon the Dragon's seat. *

Their sun to darkness turning, †
    Their moon changing to blood,
Their heav'ns arrayed in mourning,
    Wrath surging like a flood.

The elements now heating
    Will burn till they consume,
New earth and heav'n creating,
    The Church's future home.

On earth is no commotion,
    Its wars have ceased to be,
Departed is the ocean ‡
    And there is no more sea!

Jehovah now upraises
    His people as His friends,
And their new song of praises
    Begins but never ends.

BETHESDA: OR, THE MIRACULOUS POOL!

John v. 2—4.   L. M.

190. Beside the pool of gospel love,
    Famed for its living wondrous power,
I watch to see the water move,
    Which does the impotent restore.

* Rev. xiii. 2.   † Mat. xxiv. 29, 30; Acts ii. 19, 20;
Rev. vi. 12—17.   ‡ Rev. xxi. 1.

The pool in *type*, well known of old,
   Near where the sheep together came,
'Twas at Bethesda, we are told,
   Where lay the wither'd, blind and lame.

An Angel on a time went down,
   And moved the water in the pool,
Then he that followed first was known
   On stepping in to be made whole!

Hence, of all kinds were gathered there,
   Waiting the water's sudden move,
And when its waters troubled were,
   Then each one for an healing strove!

But now this pool is known within,
   In vain we may look outward now,
It's here the soul is washed from sin,
   And here the living waters flow.

Here only is the true sheep's gate,
   Here only is the living pool,
Here should the sick together wait
   To know the healing of the soul.

The Angel, too, is always nigh
   Who does the healing water move,
Then may I watch with single eye,
   And wait its living pow'rs to prove.

BETHESDA: OR, THE MIRACULOUS POOL!
    John v. 2—4.   S.M.

191. Before Bethesda's pool,
   A *type* in days of yore,
I watch to see the waters roll,
   And wait to find a cure.

   Nor am I there alone,
     Believing that it saves,
   A multitude have thither gone
     And proved its healing waves!

The wither'd, halt and blind
　　All in her porches lay,
Hoping that they a cure may find
　　Before they go their way.

Here come the living sheep,
　　Their gate is by the pool,
Here all the sick together keep
　　Waiting to be made whole.

This pool is found within,
　　Where living waters roll,
As these alone will cleanse from sin,
　　And these will heal the soul!

But I am weary grown,
　　Waiting so long in vain,
While many first have hasten'd down
　　And well returned again.

Oh! if the Angel wait,
　　Then may I tarry too,
Whene'er He comes it's not too late,
　　A word from Him will do.

CHRIST THE LIVING SPIRITUAL BREAD.

　　　　John vi. 48—58.　　　　7's & 6's.

192. Jesus, risen from the dead,
　　　　And seen go up to heav'n,
　　Is Himself the living bread
　　　　To all believers giv'n.

　　All that do in Him believe,
　　　　According to His word,
　　They shall life from Him receive,
　　　　Their ever living Lord.

He by blood and water came,*
 Which is a mystery!
There's salvation in His name
 For ev'ry sinner free!

And if we, the savèd are
 By water and by blood,
We, the life of angels share,
 Who ever live with God.

CHRIST THE BREAD OF LIFE.
John vi. 48—58.   C. M.

193. As Jesus is the living bread,
 Which cometh down from heav'n,
To those that shall upon it feed
 The hidden life is giv'n.

Partakers of His flesh and blood,
 They draw their life from thence
As spiritually understood,
 But in no carnal sense!

It's by His spirit and His grace
 By which He doth appear,
That they His promises embrace,
 And know their Saviour near.

They live by faith on Him alone,
 And know His saving power,
In mystic fellowship as one,
 Both now and evermore!

SPIRITUAL LIFE RECEIVED THROUGH FAITH IN CHRIST IS ONLY KNOWN WITHIN.
John vii. 37—39.   C. M.

194. In heart alone can we believe †
 On Jesus Christ the Lord,
And by true faith alone receive
 The living saving Word.

---

* 1 John v. 6—8; John xix. 34.   † Rom. x. 10; Jas. i. 21.

In heart we seek the Holy One,
  He who will meet us there,
Where He will give, and where alone
  The living waters are.

The living water He will give
  To those that trust in Him,
Which as His loved ones they receive,
  Is like a flowing stream.

He that doth on the Saviour call
  And wait His grace to know,
" Rivers of living water shall
  Out of his belly flow."

Those waters like a stream shall be,
  Whose springs will never cease
Their swell to all eternity,
  And in their swell increase.

To everlasting life they rise,
  Life in its essence pure,
Like their great source in paradise
  Where saints will thirst no more!

THE SAVIOUR'S GRACIOUS INVITATION AND PROMISE.

John vii. 37—39. 7's & 6's.

195. What said He, who was the first, *
      And He who is the last?
    That if any man did thirst
      He need not longer fast.

   Let him come to Me and take
     The water I will give,
   His soul's thirst with water slake,
     And drink that he may live!

* Rev. i. 8, 11.

He that doth believe in Me,
  As scripture it will show,
Out of him eternally
  Shall living waters flow!

This He of the Spirit spake,
  Which all that do believe,
For His name and mercy's sake
  Will evermore receive!

PETITION.
John xvi. 23.   S.M.

196. Unto our prayers attend
  Through Jesus offered up,
He is our Advocate and Friend,
  Our only solid hope.

No other hope have we,
  No other trust beside,
No other plea but Christ and He
  For us was crucified.

Through Him we now presume
  Thy sacred courts to tread,
We in Thy gracious presence come
  And for Thy mercy plead.

Hear Thou our one request,
  And purge our guilt away,
Our weary spirits toil for rest,
  And wait the welcome day.

"WHAT IS TRUTH?"
John xviii. 38.   7's.

197. What is truth? one asked of old,
  And if he had deigned to wait,
He who does all truth unfold,
  Would He not have answered it?

Jesus is himself the truth,*
   He alone all truth can show,
Is it not from His own mouth
   We all truth must learn and know?

Happy they who truth shall own,
   For it healing virtue gives,
'Tis the plant of great renown †
   Which for ever grows and thrives.

It is truth that lets us see
   What our state by nature is,
Truth it is which makes us free,
   And doth grant a full release.

Truth will dissipate our night,
   Which has oft caused us to stray;
Truth will be our *lamp of light* ‡
   To lead on our heav'nly way!

Truth will show us ev'rything §
   It is needful we should know;
Truth will our salvation bring,
   And a crown of life bestow!

NO SALVATION ONLY IN THE NAME OF THE LORD!

Acts iv. 12.   8's.

198. The name of the Lord is His pow'r,
   The name of the Lord is His grace;
The name of the Lord's a strong tow'r,
   The righteous run into this place.‖

His name is His judgment and might,
   Understanding and wisdom also;
His name is His love and His light,
   By which all His people must go.

---

* John xiv. 6.   † Eze. xxxiv. 29.   ‡ Prov. vi. 23.
   § 1 John ii. 27.   ‖ Pro. xviii. 10.

His name, too, is holiness shown,
   His name it is spirit and life;
In His name salvation is known,
   In which all confiders are safe.

True knowledge and wisdom are giv'n
   To those who have in it believed;
There's no other name under heav'n
   By which endless life is received.

PRAYING FOR THE ILLUMINATION AND SALVATION OF THE GENTILES.

Acts xiii. 47; John i. 6—9.　　　　L.M.

199. Shine from Thy sacred seat, O Lord,
   Let heathen nations own Thy sway;
To them both light and life afford,
   And turn their darkness into day.

Begin Thy universal reign,*
   The utmost bounds of earth possess;
Thy government o'er all maintain,
   And fill the world with righteousness.

CONVICTION OF SIN AND THE MEANS OF DELIVERANCE.

Acts xvi. 30, 31.　　　　7's & 6's.

200. Guilty, helpless, and distressed,
   Beneath a load of sin;
Whither shall I get released
   From all this mental pain?

Whither flee t' escape the wrath,
   Which hanging o'er my head,
By its gloomy aspect hath
   Now fill'd my soul with dread?

* Zech. xiv. 9.

Sure I hear the Saviour speak,
  He bids me come to Him,
That He may these fetters break
  And me from death redeem.

Save me from iniquity
  By His redeeming grace;
And in truth and equity
  Restore my soul in peace.

That He may His love declare,
  Unmerited and free;
Me, the chief of sinners, spare,
  Salvation's work to see.

Raise from sin and wrath and hell,
  And misery beneath,
That I of His love may tell,
  Freed from the second death.

Let the promise now made good,
  And the assurance giv'n:
By the strong attesting blood,
  Confirm my hope of heav'n.

Now fulfil Thy faithful word,
  Let th' blessing now take place:
Speak me into life restor'd,
  And save me by Thy grace.

THE MANDATE OF HEAVEN!
Acts xvii. 30; John iii. 18—21. 8's.

201. The Lord the commandment hath giv'n,
  That all men repent and believe,
If they would inherit His heav'n,
  And th' pearl of His favor receive.

Nor hath He commanded in vain,
  But will by His spirit afford
The grace which is needful to men,
  To repent in obeying His word.

His grace He on them will bestow,
　　Who in turning from ev'ry ill,
Shall seek Him in person to know,
　　By submitting themselves to His will.

He will not by absolute force
　　Compel them to stoop to His grace ;
For justice will act in due course,
　　If they will not His mercy embrace.

And should they, despising His rod,
　　Reject this His message conveyed,
Yet they must surrender to God,
　　He speaks and He will be obeyed.

So sure if they will not submit
　　To obey Him while here they may dwell,
Will, to their eternal regret,
　　Obey His just mandate in hell.

Not one is so hardened in sin,
　　But he will be forced at the last
To repent and be troubled in vain,
　　When th' tidings of mercy are past.

Oh, let us be wise then to know
　　When th' grace of salvation is giv'n,*
That we by embracing it now,
　　May secure a mansion in heav'n.

CONFESSION.

"God commandeth all men everywhere to repent."

Acts xvii. 30, 31.　　　　S. M.

202. The message of our God
　　　We thankfully receive ;
　　We hear and bow unto the rod,
　　　And penitently grieve.

* Tit. ii. 11—14 ; 2 Pet. iii. 9, 15.

We would not hide our sin,
　　　　But full confession make;
　　And from the present hour begin
　　　　Our follies to forsake.

　　　We hear Thy warning word,
　　　　And ask Thy kind relief;
　　We would believe Thy promise, Lord,
　　　　Save us from unbelief.

　　　Thou art the God of power,
　　　　Thou art the God of love;
　　And all Thy promises are sure,
　　　　And ever faithful prove.

　　　Save now by Thy right hand
　　　　The outcasts of Thy flock,
　　And make our feet securely stand
　　　　On the eternal rock!

　　　Through Jesus Christ the Just,
　　　　Th' repentant sinner's friend,
　　We in Thy boundless mercy trust,
　　　　And on Thy truth depend.

　　　Only unto Thy praise,
　　　　Thy glory here below,
　　Thy humble suppliants upraise,
　　　　Thy great salvation show.

　　　Make bare Thy holy arm,
　　　　By living witnesses,
　　And by an act of grace perform
　　　　Thy faithful promises.

THE GOSPEL.
Rom. i. 16.　　　　　　　L. M.

203. The Gospel is the power of God,
　　　As His true messengers declare:
　　His saving power on them bestow'd,
　　　Whose living witnesses they are!

It is the power of God to save,
   That those who servants are to sin,
May through His grace dominion have,
   When guided by His light within!

It is the glory of the Lord,
   Through earth beneath and heav'n above;
Angels rejoice with pure accord,
   And chant the theme that God is love!

It is the wonder of the wise,
   Which shows it is in part conceal'd;
Angels behold with longing eyes,*
   Till th' whole mystery be reveal'd.

The gospel message comes to tell
   The love of God to fallen man:
By saving him from wrath and hell,
   His merciful redeeming plan.

By gospel grace sinners are freed
   From the dread pains of mental strife;
It gives them all the good they need,
   Translating them from death to life.

Then 'tis good news of grace unknown
   That brings salvation unto man;
O may eternal praises crown
   The author of the gospel plan.

THE TRUE OR SPIRITUAL JEW!

Rom. ii. 28, 29.   L. M.

204. He is the true and living Jew,
   Who in his heart and mind is one;
The carnal Jew he only knew,
   And trusted in the *rites* alone.

---

* 1 Pet. i. 12.

True circumcision is of God,
　Or where the Spirit's work is known,
All such in wisdom's ways have trod,
　Their faith was by obedience shown!

The righteous Jew he lives by faith,
　By such the will of God is done,
His people whom the spirit saith,
　Worship and serve the holy One.

They glorify the Lord below,
　While life on earth to them is giv'n,
The grace which brings salvation know
　And walk and point the road to heav'n!

MAN'S MORTALITY AND SICKNESS THE EFFECTS OF SIN.

Rom. vi. 23; Isa. i. 5, 6.　　　　S. M.

205. How frail we mortals are,
　　How subject to decay,
Pains and infirmities declare
　　By a perpetual stay.

　　Sickness of ev'ry kind
　　Attends our mortal state,
Our days unto a period wind,
　　And fix their worthless date.

　　Just like a spreading taint,
　　Human disorders come,
The creatures with themselves acquaint
　　And point their journey home!

　　Soon as we draw our breath,
　　We draw it in disease,
Nor till we close our eyes in death
　　Will its infection cease.

Thus all are trav'lling in
  Their courses to the grave,
They pay the penalty of sin,
  And none a ransom have. *

Then as we know that all
  Will there together meet,
Let us walk in the way that shall
  Make the remembrance sweet.

May we consider well
  That away th' spirit flies,
And must exist in heav'n or hell
  Soon as the body dies.

In those eternal states,
  Whichever this succeeds,
Our happiness or misery waits
  According to our deeds.

THE SAINT'S PROSPECT OF FUTURE BLESSEDNESS.

1 Cor. ii. 9—13   4-6's & 2-8's.

206. Not mortal eye hath seen,
  Nor mortal ear hath heard,
Nor heart acquainted been
  With things God hath prepar'd
For those that do Him fear and love,
And faithful in His service move!

Deep hidden and concealed,
  To all the world unknown,
They only are revealed
  To those nam'd as His own;
For they are by the Spirit shown,
And by His light to them made known.

* Psa. xlix. 7, 8.

Thus, as they Him receive,
 To take Him as their guide,
And in the Spirit live,
 Nor from Him turn aside,
He showeth unto them all things, *
And knowledge of the future brings!

Such of those things may speak,
 As they empower'd are,
For they inwardly seek
 And learn their duty there;
They know the Spirit them to lead,
And are accepted in their Head.

THE SPIRITUAL PASSOVER!

1 Cor. v. 7, 8.

207. Christ, our passover, is slain,
 Sacrificed for ev'ry guest,
He hath died and rose again,
 Therefore let us keep the feast.

The old leaven now forsake,
 Not on sin and malice feed,
But by living faith partake
 Of the true unleavened bread!

All partake the heav'nly food,
 And the cup which Angels love
Ever spiritually good,
 Coming from the Lord above.

He our Saviour condescends
 Then to make Himself a guest,
Maketh joyful all His friends,
 And with blessings crowns the feast.

* John xvi. 13 and 1 John ii. 20, 27.

THE HEAVENLY RACE.

1 Cor. ix. 24. 6 lines 8's.

208. Now while the sun shines clear and bright,
And it supplies the day with light,
May I pursue my heav'nly course;
   For when o'er me the night shall come,
   I'm not within the reach of home,
Darkness will make the journey worse.

I also then might lose my way,
Might from the path of duty stray,
And so might miss of heav'n at last;
   The glass of life will soon be run,
   And then appears the setting sun,
Therefore I cannot move too fast.

THE ANTITYPE!

"That Rock was Christ."

1 Cor. x. 4. 7's.

209. Jesus is the living Rock,
Which the rod of God hath struck,
And from Him the waters fall,
Which He giveth unto all.

He doth living water give,
And of Him we drink and live,
Who our living Rock will be
Unto all eternity.

TEMPTATIONS.

1 Cor. x. 13; Jas. i. 2, 12. S. M.

210. Thou watcher of my soul,
   Whose eyes can never sleep,
Arise, the boistr'ous waves control,
   And still the raging deep.

My wand'ring spirit flies
  Down to the gates of hell;
Again with earnestness she tries
  To break the evil spell.

Lord, Thou hast search'd me through,
  And seen my inmost mind;
Thou know'st my wand'rings to and fro,
  Unsettled as the wind.

In darkness and distress
  I heard Thy secret call,
Which showed me all my wretchedness,
  Nor suffered me to fall.

Help me to look to Thee,
  And trust Thy power to save,
That I may Thy salvation see,
  And safe deliv'rance have.

It is by Thy free grace,
  Solely in mercy giv'n,
That I may hope to see Thy face,
  And find true rest in heav'n.

THE RESURRECTION.

1 Cor. xv. 35—44.   4-6's & 2-8's.

211. And must this body die
    And sink in the low grave,
  There hushed in silence lie,
    Without a hand to save;
In Death's cold icy grasp to stay
Till the great resurrection day,

  When it must rise again;
    Yea, pure, immortal, be,
  And nature burst the chain
    Of dead mortality,
And sin and death be purg'd away
In the great resurrection day!

When it to earth goes down,
    To hide from mortal eyes,
It is in weakness sown,
    But it in pow'r shall rise;
With its dishonor swept away,
In the great resurrection day!

This life it doth forsake
    To end a painful strife;
But then it shall awake
    To everlasting life:
And glory its new form array
In the great resurrection day!

Then what are all our toils,
    Our pains and suff'rings now,
If we must gather spoils
    From all our griefs below?
If earth must recompense our stay
In the great resurrection day?

Then let us hope and wait,
    And patiently contend:
Our harvest will be great,
    And glorious in the end;
For heav'n will all things us repay
In the great resurrection day!

THE TRANSLATIONS!

Gen. v. 24; 2 Kings ii. 11.

Enoch before the Law had gone!
    Under the Law Elijah went!
In Gospel times will there be none?
    Or what is by th' Mystery meant?

A MYSTERY!
1 Cor. xv. 51, 52.
L. M.

212. God's spirit shows a mystery ;
    A sudden change wrought by His Word,
Shall in the twinkling of an eye,
    Be at the coming of the Lord !

For His own people will not sleep,
    Who then upon the earth are found ;
But their rewards in life will reap
    When the *last trump* of God shall sound !

The trumpet's voice will wake the dead,
    When from their graves He calls His own,
That He their righteous cause may plead,
    And them with grace and glory crown !

His prophets then He will reward,
    With all that fear Him small and great,
Who for His coming are prepar'd,
    And now with joy their Saviour meet.

They reign with Him a thousand years !
    Then truth will flourish in the earth ;
Prosperity will wipe their tears,
    And righteousness and praise spring forth.

The former troubles are no more,
    Now all the nations are as one ;
God reigns in love on ev'ry shore,
    And they all worship Him alone !

ALL GOD'S PROMISES ARE SURE.
2 Cor. i. 20.
7's.

213. Many are the promises
    Given to us by the Lord ;
If we did believe in these,
    Would He not perform His word ?

True and faithful is our God,
   And whatever He shall speak,
He most surely will make good
   Who His word can never break.

Come we then unto His throne,
   Never in this duty fail;
Plead His righteousness alone,
   With this plea we shall prevail!

Ask of Him whate'er we will,
   We can never ask too much:
He that doth His word fulfil,
   Giveth freely unto such.

Giving doth not make Him poor,
   Nor withholding make Him rich:
For He is an open door,
   Where a change can never reach.

All created things are His,
   Through immensity of space,
With its endless treasuries,
   Everlasting stores of grace!

CHRIST THE HEAD OF HIS CHURCH!

Eph. i. 20—23 and v. xxiii; Col. i. 18.   7's & 6's.

214. Jesus of His Church is Head,
   And Ruler of the same;
Mortals who this pow'r may plead,
   Falsely assume the name.

   He's the Head of ev'ry man
      In His true Church below;
   Christians led by Jesus can
      No other leader know!

He their great Commander is,*
  Witness and Leader too ;
All commands opposed to His
  They safely may forego.

Thrones and principalities
  Before His footstool fall ;
He alone their Maker is,
  And Ruler of them all !

SAVING FAITH KNOWN BY ITS FRUITS.
Eph. ii. 8—10. C. M.

215. It is through faith that we are saved,
  Our works cannot atone,
The *principle* must be received
  Before *right* works are done !

Yet he that doth *good* works decry †
  Knoweth not what he saith,
For they as clearly justify
  Being the fruits of faith !

For neither separate can save,
  They cannot life afford,
And those who this great blessing have,
  Received it from the Lord.

Yet faith is one condition made ‡
  And works a kindred mean,
Whereby salvation must be had
  Upon the gospel plan.

And these as one together go,
  Nor can we ever find,
That they can separation know
  Which are so closely join'd.

* Isa. lv. 4.   † Isa. xxvi. 12.   ‡ Jas. ii. 20—26.

Still Christ is the First Cause of all,
It's through His own shed blood
We now receive the grace, and shall
For ever live with God!

GOD IN HIS *TRIUNE* POWER MAKING PROVISION FOR MAN'S SALVATION.

Eph. iii. 9—11; 1 Pet. i. 18—20.   L. M.

216. God He foresaw the fall of man,
And felt His yearning pity move,
Devised His great redeeming plan
In gracious, everlasting love.

Jesus vouchsafed Himself to give
A sacrifice made free for all,
That those who should in Him believe,
Might be recovered from the fall.

The Holy Spirit by His power—
This is His work and His alone—
A holy nature does restore,
And take away the heart of stone.

And yet it is conditional
That all the promises are giv'n,
That we may do His will withal,
And be on earth made meet for heav'n.

THE GREAT POWER OF GOD, BY HIS SPIRIT, WITHIN US.

Eph. iii. 20.   S. M.

217. Almighty God of love,
Thy inward living power
Will to the saints salvation prove
Both now and evermore.

And if they firmly trust
And fully in it dwell,
Then they, with all their fathers, must
Its signs and wonders tell.

CIRCUMSPECTION.

Ephe. v. 15.

218. Be circumspect in your talk,
Be upright in all your walk,
Let your words and actions prove
That you circumspectly move.

Be careful in whom you trust,
Be in all your dealings just,
Always unto others do
As you think they should to you!

If you see a neighbor wrong
Do not slander with the tongue;
If you cannot hide a fault,
Yet from evil speaking halt;

If you see one in distress,
Help to make his suff'rings less;
Cheer the spirit that is sad,
Strive to make the humble glad.

Kindness will to many be
Evidence of charity:
Thus religion understood
Will appear a solid good.

Then let all you do or say,
In the darkness or the day,
Yourselves wise as serpents prove
And as harmless as the dove!

THE DYING BELIEVER'S PRAYER.
Phil. i. 23.

219. Come, my Saviour, quickly come,
To receive thy wand'rer home,
In Thy chariot, paved with love,
Bear me to Thyself above.

My poor fainting heart revive,
Let Thy dying creature live,
Cleanse, O cleanse me with Thy blood,
Make me meet to live with God.

Fetch me, Jesus, where Thou art,
Freely I with all things part,
Let me now Thy glory see,
For I long to be with Thee.

Come, my Saviour, come, I pray,
Come and bear my soul away,
Unto me, through grace be giv'n,
Everlasting rest in heav'n.

"REJOICE IN THE LORD ALWAYS."
Phil. iv. 4.

220. Let th' servants of Jesus rejoice,
Supported and governed by Him,
They cheerfully wait on His voice,
And live in His blessed esteem.

His love more abundantly shown
Will its richest effusions distil,
On them it shall all be made known
Who th' works of His pleasure fulfil

A present salvation from sin,
　　Believing in Him they enjoy;
But then without sorrow or pain,
　　And bliss without any alloy.

Their fruit they to holiness bear,
　　And O what a glorious end,
In th' presence of God to appear,
　　And th' life of eternity spend.

ANTICHRIST.

2 Thess. ii. 3—12.　　　　　S's & 7's.

Him who after Satan cometh
　　With a seeming pious zeal,
And a sanctity assumeth
　　His deceptions to conceal.

By false signs and lying wonders
　　He leads many souls astray!
And doth fulminate his thunders
　　Should they cease to own his sway.

As by a self-exaltation
　　He doth show himself as God!
So, by a most strange dictation,
　　He doth rule with iron rod.

By his sorceries alluring*
　　Blinded souls beneath his yoke,
They his servitude enduring
　　And his favor they invoke.

But the Lord is him consuming,
　　By those means he doth employ,
And whose brightness at His coming,
　　Him will utterly destroy!

* False doctrines, Rev. xviii. 23; Acts xiii. 6—8.

May this voice of timely warning
    All the captivated hear,
So that they of Jesus learning
    Him alone may serve and fear!

That they may escape the judgment,
    Which the world will surely know,
And survive the day of vengeance
    In his final overthrow.

"ONE MEDIATOR!"

1 Tim. ii. 5, 6; Acts iv. 12.

222. Th' Bible speaks of a mediator,
    One alone we read is giv'n,
Who is man's conciliator,
    With the majesty of heav'n.

It has only of one spoken,
    Seeking others surely must
Be to such the plainest token,
    They do not in Jesus trust.

How should men needing redemption,
    Who but redeem'd sinners are,
Claim the grace of mediation,
    And the Saviour's glory share?

If of grace they are possessors,
    Through the mercy of the Lord,
Shall we make them intercessors,
    Beyond warrant from his word?

Ev'ry gracious act or favor
    We for them could ever claim,
Is through *merits* of the Saviour,
    And they give the praise to Him!

There no other name is given,
   As the spirit doth record,
For salvation under heaven,
   But the name of Christ the Lord !

RELIGION THE SOURCE OF TRUE AND LASTING HAPPINESS.

1 Tim. 4, 8.   C. M.

223. Religion makes our happiness
   While in this world below,
And trav'lling through the wilderness
   That better state to know.

The promise of this life it has
   Also of that to come,
By this bright hope we onward pass
   To our unfading home !

It's but a taste, which here we have
   Of mental happiness,
Compared with that beyond the grave,
   We shall in heaven possess.

How great that bliss no one can tell,*
   And Scripture hath declar'd
It doth all human thought excel,
   And is the saint's reward.

Pleasures are there without decline,
   Of most refined delight,
There glories in perfection shine
   Exquisite to the sight.

Felicities unknown by faith
   Eternity employs,
Where spirits are transported with
   Uninterrupted joys !

* 1 Cor. ii. 9.

MAN'S SUPREMACY IN THE WORKS OF CREATION!

Heb. ii. 6—8. L. M.

224. Lord, what is man whom Thou hast made
To place o'er all Thy works as head:
That Thou hast magnified him so,
And set Thy heart upon him too?

To Thee it was both good and meet
All things to put beneath his feet,
Of all below and all above
The brightest image of Thy love!

INVITATION.

Heb. iii. 7—11. C. M.

225. Now in the Day of Christ the Lord
   If ye His voice will hear,
Who doth His *inward light* afford
   By which He doth appear!

Do not as Israel disobey,
   When they the desert trod,
Who to temptations fell a prey
   And sinn'd against their God;

For there the tribes were overthrown,
   Who the commandments broke,
Although they had deliv'rance known
   From the Egyptian yoke.

The glorious gospel of the Lord*
   Was also preach'd to them,
The gospel of the *living* Word,
   Who does the soul redeem!

* Heb. iv. 2.

Yet the Word preach'd was but in vain
  To those who disbelieved;
They heard to murmur and complain,
  And thus the Spirit grieved.

Wherefore it was in wrath exprest,
  And sworn by the great God,
They should not enter in His rest
  Who thus provoked His rod.

They fell by unbelief and sin
  While in the wilderness,
None but the faithful entered in,
  Who did the land possess.

And now the heav'nly Rest remains *
  The faithful souls' reward,
The rest of love where Jesus reigns,
  The Sabbath of the Lord †

INVITATION.

Heb. iv. 7—11.   S. M.

226. To-day if ye will hear
  The voice of Christ the Lord,
Who doth not outwardly appear,
  But is th' ingrafted Word, ‡

Then harden not your hearts,
  Nor dare resist His grace,
Who heav'nly *light* and *life* imparts
  To all the earth-born race!

Then hearken to His voice,
  Attend His *inward* call,
That you may in His love rejoice,
  Who offers it to all!

* Heb. iv. 9, 10.   † Zeph. iii. 17.   ‡ Jam. i. 21.

The soul that heareth Him,
  And learns of Him alone,
Shall know His power to redeem
  When other helps are gone !

Poor sinners that receive
  His invitation giv'n,
Shall hear His quick'ning voice and live
  On earth the life of heav'n.

He does the weary save
  And make them wise and blest :
In Him they life eternal have
  And everlasting rest !

THE TYPICAL SABBATH.

Heb. iv. 4; Gen. ii. 2, 3 ; Exo. xx. 9—11 and xxxi. 12—17 ;
Eze. xx. 12 ; Col. ii. 16, 17.   S. M.

227. The Sabbath was a type
  Of the pure heav'nly rest,
In Jesus Christ the anti-type
  Believers have possest !

The Sabbath of the Jews,
  By God ordain'd of old,
To those who did it rightly use,
  This holy rest foretold !

Also old Canaan's land,
  By Israel possest,
As we may plainly understand,
  A type was of this rest !

As in six days alone
  By the Almighty Word,
The whole creation's work was done
  And Paradise restor'd.

  To those that enter in
   The Sabbath of the Lord,*
  Shall the eternal rest begin
   His light and love afford!

  For all that do believe
   May enter into rest,
  Which they in Jesus Christ receive,
   And be for ever blest!

THE ANTI-TYPICAL SABBATH!

Heb. iv. 9, 10; Isa. lxvi. 23, margin.

228. The Sabbath is God's day of rest,
  Cause me, O Lord, to find it so;
 And make me feel divinely blest
  In all I think, or speak, or do.

Day of the Lord, spiritual day,†
  In which alone true rest is found;
 Where all the *signs* are done away,
  And light, and life, and joy abound!

The Sabbath was a type of old,
  And unto those that knew their signs,
 The heav'nly rest in Christ foretold,
  Which now eternally remains!

The fruitful and delightsome land
  Of Canaan shadow'd forth this rest,
 (The heav'nly Canaan, understand)
  Where saints will be for ever blest.

The types and shadows thence are flown,
  There signs and symbols ever cease,
 Only realities are known,
  Which will true happiness increase!

---

* Isa. lxvi. 23. see margin; Heb. iv. 9. † Rev. i. 10;
  2 Cor. i. 14; 1 Thes. v. 5.

The SUBSTANCE of them all is there
By souls in Paradise possest;
Perfection reigneth ev'rywhere,
Fruition of a glorious rest!

THE OUTWARD TABERNACLE WITH ITS SERVICES, TYPIFIED THE SPIRITUAL TABERNACLE OR SANCTUARY OF GOD!

Heb. ix. 1—12, and viii. 1, 2.   8's.

229. When th' Tab'rnacle was erected,
Its parts and dimensions were giv'n;
And when the whole were perfected,
They were *patterns* of things in heav'n.

The *types* were wrought with precision,
As Moses, instructed of God,
First saw repr'sented in vision,
When on Horeb's mountain he stood.*

Those *types* were famous in story,
They furnished their lessons of old;
But their *anti-types* in glory,
The privileged alone behold!

The curtain of separation
Divided the building with care:
In th' first, with due preparation,
The priests in its services share.

But into th' second division,
The High Priest he entered alone,
And yearly, on each occasion,
Did for all past errors atone.

But the last High Priest appointed,
Who hath entered within the veil,
Is Jesus the Lord's anointed,
Whose atonement can never fail!†

* Ex. xxv. 40, and xxvi. 30; Heb. viii. 5.
† Heb. ix. 24—26, and x. 19—23.

THE OFFERINGS AND SACRIFICES UNDER THE LAW, FORESHADOWED THE *ONE* OFFERING AND SACRIFICE BY JESUS CHRIST, OF HIMSELF, FOR SIN !

Heb. x. 1—14.   7's.

230. While the Tabernacle stood
    For the service of the Lord,
With its offerings of blood,
    That were on the altar pour'd,

The off'rings a meaning had,
    Each one its instruction brings,
Which the worshippers forbad
    Then to trust in earthly things,

Each pointed to One above,
    And His great redeeming plan,
Who, in mercy and in love,
    Offered up Himself for man !

Jesus, the pure Lamb of God,
    From the world's foundation slain—
He hath shed His precious blood,
    And from death hath ris'n again.

All should now in Him believe,
    Who the Saviour is of all !*
Who will freely them receive,
    And restore them from the fall.

If in Him alone we trust,
    And His promises embrace,
He, our great deliv'rer, must
    Own His work of saving grace.

* 1 Tim. iv. 10 ; 1 John ii. 2

FAITH AND PATIENCE NECESSARY IN ORDER TO FINAL PERSEVERANCE.

Heb. x. 35, 36. L. M.

231. Patience is needful to the saints,
  As it will keep them from offence;
But he that staggers, tires and faints,
  Will cast away his confidence.

Yes, he will cast that *pearl* away,
  Which God doth from on high regard;
To fatal snares become a prey,
  And lose the blessings of reward.

Nor should we treat as needless fears,
  What we may evidently know:
For Christ th' unerring witness bears,*
  And doth the consequence foreshow.

He gives us, then, His warning word,
  That we may timely caution take:
Stand fast, believing in the Lord,
  And sure our own election make.†

Lord, grant us wisdom to foresee
  The dangers that beset our path;
And closely knit our souls to Thee
  By all the pow'r and life of faith.

Lord, by Thy free, preserving grace,
  Lead Thy dependent creatures on,
Until we meet before Thy face,
  And realise Salvation won.

"THE BLOOD OF SPRINKLING WHICH SPEAKETH BETTER THINGS THAN THAT OF ABEL!"

Heb. xii. 24. L. M.

232. When Abel his first off'ring made,‡
  It did with pure acceptance rise;
Which shows the confidence he had
  In the *prefigured* Sacrifice!

---

* John xv. 1—6.   † 2 Pet. i. 10.   ‡ Gen. iv. 4.

God had respect unto his faith,
  And so receiv'd the off'ring brought :
For such a favor plainly saith,
  That Abel His *free mercy* sought !

And here we see the Spirit's mind,*
  How, or of what his off'ring spake —
That all who would acceptance find,
  They must of Abel's faith partake !

But Jesus see His own blood brings,
  Himself is made the sacrifice ;
It therefore speaks of better things,
  As faith the offering applies !

It speaks of mercy unto all,
  Or any of the human race,
Who shall in faith upon Him call,
  And so accept of His *free* grace.

It speaks of better things above,
  Of never-ending joys to come ;
Speaks of a pure, undying love,
  And of an everlasting home !

THE SHORTNESS OF TIME !

Jas. i. 10 and iv. 14.

233. How swift and hasty is our life,
  How rapidly it flies ;
'Tis but a momentary strife,
  And in a moment dies.

The subject of a thousand cares,
  The creature winds his breath ;
In thoughtless vanity he shares,
  And little thinks of death.

* Heb. xi. 4.

A year, a month, a week, a day,
   Yea, in a single hour,
Man may be summon'd hence away,
   And here be seen no more.

Then, what is done remaineth done,
   It cannot altered be;
The time for this has fled and gone,
   Into eternity.

If he, through grace, has acted well,
   The soul will rest in heav'n;
If without grace, it sinks to hell,*
   And is to darkness driv'n.

Then let us number the few days †
   Which we on earth may spend;
That we may walk in wisdom's ways,
   And keep them to the end.

GOOD WORKS THE EVIDENCE OF TRUE AND SAVING FAITH!

Jas. ii. 20—26.‡   S. M.

234. Faith without works is dead;
   And as the body, when
Its *living principle* has fled,
   No more to come again!

Just as the shell is found,
   Soon as the kernel dies;
Or like the shadow on the ground,
   Wherein no substance is!

From such a faith as this,
   Good Lord, deliver us;
Give us the faith that genuine is,
   The faith victorious.

---

* Psa. xlix. 19, see margin.   † Psa. xc. 12.
‡ Isa. xxvi. 12; Eph. ii. 8—10.

The faith that life imparts,
   And doth to sight improve :
The faith that ruleth in our hearts,
   And always works by love !*

"DEATH AND LIFE ARE IN THE POWER OF THE TONGUE."

James iii. 2—8 ; Prov. xviii. 21.   L. M.

235. How full of evil is the tongue,
   Yea, of iniquity how full ;
Its baneful tendency is strong,
   Corrupting to the very soul.

It is a fire, whose burning force
   No human stratagem can quell ;
It sets on fire all nature's course,
   And it is set on fire of hell !

Nothing but sov'reign grace can tame
   This deadly and destroying thing,
Modify it with purer flame,
   That life may from its action spring,†

Yea, make it as a tree of life,‡
   That ministers to those around ;
A softener of human strife,
   Which through transgression doth abound.

This change will make the humble glad,
   For soon its benefits they find :
Who see it now as useful made,
   Promoting peace among mankind.

Its benign services are good,
   And salutary influence yield ;
This, by their fruit is understood,
   Which men's approval have compell'd.

---

* Gal. v. 6.   † Prov. x. 11.   ‡ Prov. xv. 4.

THE RESURRECTION OF CHRIST MAN'S HOPE OF GLORY.

1 Pet. i. 3—5.   8's.

236. He is ris'n again from the dead,
    Who once was on Calvary slain;
Our Saviour, our Prince, and our Head,
    Is seated in glory again!

He once for His people hath died,
    To give them assurance of bliss;
His callèd, His chosen, and tried,
    That they may His kingdom possess.

They may be despisèd and poor,
    As He, their great pattern, hath been;
Yet Heaven has open'd its door,
    And grace and salvation are seen.

And they, when they 'ave ended their race,
    Shall into those mansions remove,
To 'inherit that happier place,
    And reign in the smiles of His love!

CHRIST (BY HIS SPIRIT) PREACHING TO THE SPIRITS IN PRISON!

1 Pet. iii. 18—20; Isa. lxi. 1.; xlii. 6, 7 and xlix. 9.   C.M.

237. Poor souls, in their dark prison-house,
    Bound with the chains of sin,
Let Thy good Spirit, Lord, arouse,
    And break their ev'ry chain.

Deliver them, by Thy great might,
    Who seem no hope to have;
And bring them forth into the light,
    To know Thy pow'r to save.

Thou only canst redeem lost souls;*
   Through Thy all-pleading blood,
Heav'n's mercy as an ocean rolls,
   Or a deluging flood!

Thou hast for the transgressors died,
   Thy saving love to show;
That sinners may be justified,
   And Thy salvation know.

The greatest rebels in thy sight,†
   May, by repentance, find
Their prison darkness changed to light,
   And leave their chains behind.

Imprisoned spirits thus may know,
   And liberty obtain,
To leave the house of sin below,
   And walk in light again!

Such may Thy vict'ries, Lord, extend,
   And spread abroad Thy fame;
Their time on earth most freely spend,
   To glorify Thy name.

THE FALL OF ANGELS.
2 Pet. ii. 4; Jude 6.   8 lines 8s.

238. No tongue can speak nor words can tell
What are the punishments of hell,
Where those unhappy spirits dwell,
Who from their state primeval fell,
And were by flaming vengeance driv'n
Down from their shining seats in heav'n.
Down from those habitations fair,
Which only treason could impair,
To grind in prisons of despair,
Where dismal voices pierce the air,
For th' house of death to them is giv'n,
Where prison bars cannot be riv'n.

---
* Luke xix. 10.   † Psa. cvii. 10—14; Mark iii. 28, 29.

How is their bliss for ever lost,
Those visages of beauty crost,
Which graced the whole satanic host,
Of highest treason made the cost!
While pride in grov'lling darkness lies,
Nor finds the ease of weeping eyes.
Thick hellish night succeeded day,
And fiery wrath their forms array;
Stern justice marked the gloomy way
And moaned for them a hopeless lay,
Records their sentence as she flies,
Whose glory thence for ever dies.

"HE THAT HATETH HIS BROTHER IS A MURDERER."

1 John iii. 15.   L. M.

239. With hatred harbored in the breast
The soul cannot with Jesus rest:
It cannot the true union know,
Whence life and happiness must flow.

Th' effectual barrier is great,
For Satan still maintains his seat;
The evil principle of sin
Predominates and rules within.

This rule of sin must be destroyed
Before religion is enjoyed,
Before it saves from death and hell
And fits the soul with God to dwell!

Against all murmurs and complaints
This truth is witness'd by the saints;
This revelation doth attest,
Nor falsehood could the truth infest.

THE IMMENSITY OF DIVINE LOVE!
1 John iv. 8.

240. Fountain of bliss, unmeasured love,
Who shall thine utmost borders prove,
Thy never-failing springs abound,
And here alone our life is found.

Here a consoling peace we find,
To ease the sorrows of the mind,
And strength according to our day,
To travel on our heav'nly way.

Here we may endless pleasures know,
Which makes our happiness below;
Here we may see our sins forgiv'n:
Here we may taste the joys of heav'n!

O bliss that swallows ev'ry thought,
That brings our senses down to nought,
Who shall the unknown limits prove
Of an immensity of love?

The mind may sink into the steep,
Yet cannot fathom all the deep;
Angelic pow'rs may rise with might,
Yet cannot grasp th' amazing height.

Or if again they try their strength
To trace the borders of its length,
It still remains an unknown wide,
Which men nor angels cannot stride!

Th' enlightened penetrating mind
May ever seek yet never find,
For mind its evidence will trace
Into illimitable space!

The Angel with his larger pow'rs,
By far exceeding those of ours,
May with a never-ending joy
A whole eternity employ!

DIVINE LOVE!
1 John iv. 8.   C. M.

241. Blest be the fountain of Thy love,
  That cheers our dying souls,
Where streams of mercy even move,
  And long salvation rolls.

Thence blessings, far beyond our thought,
  Are gliding gently down,
Yet seldom hath our senses wrought
  To take them for our own.

Did we but watch at wisdom's gates *
  And at her doorposts stay,
As in the night the watchman waits
  And looks for break of day;

Nor leave this post as if too strait,
  Which all the living trod,
But though the promise tarry wait
  Until it speak from God.

Our morning, too, would surely break,
  Yea, in full lustre shine,
And the Eternal to us speak
  In language all divine!

His lessons should we learn and know,
  Who ever lives above,
And by His grace and goodness show
  The praises of His love!

GOD IS LOVE!
1 John iv. 8, 16.   4-8's & 2-6's.

242. My soul mounts up on eagle's wings,
  And unto Thee, my God, she sings
    With an enlivened strain:

* Prov. viii. 34—36; Psa. cxxx. 5, 6.

Drawn by the lure of strong desire,
The sacred flame of heav'nly fire,
   She thus renews her strain.

She worships Thee, Almighty Power,
And doth Thy Majesty adore,
   Which glorious is in praise:
Rejoicing in that matchless love,
Which fires the Seraphim above
   In their immortal lays!

Love is the burden of their song,
It moves their rapt'rous strains along
   With increasing delight:
Spirits behold with longing eyes,
And grace is pour'd in rich supplies
   To raise the bliss in height!

My God, Thy loving pow'rful name,
Inspires them with the living flame
   Of an unequalled joy:
My soul would join their harmony,
And in the worshipping of Thee
   A holy song employ.

THE *TRIUNE* FOUNDATION OF THE FAITH, CONFIDENCE, AND SECURITY OF TRUE CHRISTIANS.

1 John v. 4—8; Ephe. iv. 4—6.   S. M.

243. True Christians know one God,
   He reigns in heav'n above;
His throne has 'eternal ages stood,
   And never can remove.

They only know one Lord,
   The source of ev'ry good,
As the one true life giving Word,
   By water and by blood.

Here faith and trust alone
  Make their salvation sure :
In Father, Word, and Spirit one,
  Both now and evermore !

THE DEVIL.

1 John v. 19.* Eccles. ix. 3. 8's & 7's.

244. Men have hearts quite full of evil,
  Madness dwells in them also ;
They are servants to the devil,
  Who will sure torment them too.

He is nam'd as the Old Serpent,
  And his terror who can tell,
In exploits of mischief fervent,
  Low in cunning, deep as hell !

See the monster arm'd and sable
  Skilled in battle great in might,
Who among us shall be able
  To engage with him in fight ?

At his sight our strength would weaken,
  At his presence should we fall,
And a prey by him be taken
  Who rejoices in our thrall !

Yet mankind are willing captives
  To this dreadful human foe,
And in all the serpent still lives
  Who frequent his ways of woe.

This sad story is a warning,
  Oh that sinners would it take,
That they may escape the burning
  In his black and fiery lake.

*The whole world lieth in wickedness; literally, "in the Wicked One."—*Clarke's Commentary.*

THE WORLD.

1 John v. 19 ; Eccles. ix. 3.   L. M.

245. How full of darkness sin and woe
    Is this vain world in which we live,
How like a flood their waves o'erflow
    And all things else before them drive.

How doth iniquity abound?
    How hath it the whole earth o'erspread?
By which mankind are sunk and drown'd
    And spiritually lost and dead.

Dead to the righteous life divine,
    The holy state man did possess
When he did in God's image shine
    And His true character express!

The sin and sorrow who can tell
    Which men have known since Adam stood,
When he in paradise did dwell
    And knew and convers'd with his God.

How bright his love, how pure its flames,
    How great the wisdom he displayed,
Who could pronounce appropriate names
    For all the creatures God had made!

Before him was the woman brought,
    From sleep he fixed his eyes on her,
His mind with inward knowledge fraught
    Did her right origin declare!

But since that time what darkness has
    Covered the whole creation round,
And he who then in glory was
    Soon in a fallen state was found.

He sinned, his offspring sunk with him
   In guilt and misery and woe;
And none but Jesus can redeem
   Then may we wait His pow'r to know.

"THE SEVEN SPIRITS OF GOD!"
Rev. i. 4, and iii. 1, and iv. 5, and v. 6.   C. M.

246. Behold the seven lamps of fire
   Burning before the throne,
Their qualities are *each* entire,
   Their band of union one!

Th' seven spirits of God are these;
   In glory and in power
Their operations never cease,
   Nor will they evermore

"THE KEY OF DAVID!"
Rev. iii. 7.   8's & 7's.

247. He who hath the key of David,
   He who shines upon the mind;
By whose light and grace the savèd,
   Knowledge pure and wisdom find

And in proof we have the tokens,
   None could be more plainly put:
"When He shutteth no man opens,
   When He opens none can shut!"

How much better is the learning
   We receive from Christ the Lord,
By His Spirit truth discerning,
   As He doth His light afford.

Let us our own ways forsaking,
   As He shall instruction give;
That of His free grace partaking,
   We may hear His voice and live!

THE CELESTIAL RAINBOW!
Rev. iv. 3; Eze. i. 28.   8's.

248. Jehovah in majesty reigns,
    Whom angelic spirits adore :
Whose praises in rapturous strains
    Are heard on the heav'nly shore.

The rainbow which *arches* the throne,
    Proclaiming life's covenant sure !
Where th' bright rays of glory have shone,
    And so will for ever endure.

The beautiful rainbow above,
    In sight like an emerald green,
Shows th' freshness of mercy and love,
    Which there in perfection are seen !

And the paradisaical feast,
    When th' full times of this world are past,
It will satiate ev'ry guest,
    And yet will eternally last.

THE CREATOR AND RULER OF ALL WORLDS!
Rev. iv. 10, 11.   L. M.

249. Great God, with trembling awe I bow
    Before Thy throne of majesty ;
Most wondrous in Thy works art Thou,
    And wondrous Thy supremacy.

Unto all worlds Thy praise extends,
    For Thou art Maker of them all ;
Thy Government their State defends,
    And by Thy power they stand or fall !

Thou art the universal King,
    The Monarch of eternity;
To Thee pertaineth ev'ry thing
    Throughout the space infinity.

Wherefore let ev'ry creature bow
   Before Thy throne of majesty:
In worlds above and worlds below,
   And own Thy just supremacy.

ASCRIBING ALL PRAISE, HONOR, POWER, AND GLORY TO GOD.

Rev. iv. 10, 11. L.M.

250. Now to the King whose power supreme
Bears up this universal frame,
Who by His unknown strength sustains
The worlds above o'er which He reigns:

To Him be praise and worship giv'n
Beyond the strains of earth and heaven,
With majesty, dominion, power,
And highest glory evermore.
                    Hallelujah.

THE SEALS.

Rev. v. 1—5. L.M.

251. The Lamb He openeth the seals
   Impressed and covered with the night,
Their wonders He alone reveals
   Who bringeth all things to the light.

The book of prophecy is sealed
   Both on the inside and the out,
By Him its myst'ries are revealed
   Whose Spirit solveth ev'ry doubt!

He openeth the seals to those
   Where He imparts the inward sight,
Their hidden meaning to disclose
   By His all pure and searching light!

And what He by the Spirit shows
  The mind is so convinced by it,
As each enlightened seeker knows
  That nothing can extinguish it.

THE LAMB WITH SEVEN HORNS AND SEVEN EYES!

Rev. v. 6.   7's & 6's.

252. The Lamb who hath seven horns
  Who holds a sev'nfold power,
Who once wore a crown of thorns
  Now reigns for evermore!

He who hath sev'n eyes of flame
  Sent through the earth abroad,
And who claims the highest name
  Upon the throne of God!

Those horns seven spirits are,
  Those eyes they are the same,
As both th' spirit doth declare
  Are seen upon the Lamb!

All praises to Him are given *
  By Angels and by men,
Both in the earth and heaven
  With the Seraphim's Amen!

The Immanuel is He,
  The God who dwelt with men,
As He will manifested be
  When He appears again.

When He deliverance brings,
  T' His Church the grace affords,
She'll praise Him as King of kings †
  And as the Lord of lords.

* Rev. v. 6—14.   † Rev. xix. 11—16.

THE ROYAL SUPREMACY OF THE LAMB!
Rev. v. 6. C.M.

253. Behold the Lamb who hath sev'en horns,
    With His sev'en eyes of flame,
The highest glory Him adorns *
    That gives the highest name!

Those horns are symbols of His power, †
    His all-prevailing might,
Those eyes will make His foes to cower ‡
    By their all-piercing sight.

For they the seven spirits are ||
    As seen before the throne,
Whose operations will declare
    Their band of union one!

He holds the *key* of mysteries, §
    And He unlocks the same,
For by the light Himself supplies,
    All revelations came!

At His command in heav'n above, ¶
    Obedient to His will,
The Angels in their courses move,
    His pleasure to fulfil.

Yet as a Lamb He ruleth those
    Who meekly own His rod, **
Who humble trust in Him repose,
    Their Saviour and their God.

THE "INNUMERABLE COMPANY OF ANGELS."
Rev. v. 11, 12; Heb. xii. 22. L.M.

254. When Angels join to praise the Lord,
    Great multitudes with one accord
    Around the throne assembled are,
    And who their number can declare?

---

* Rev. xvii. 18.   † Rev. vi. 16.   ‡ Heb. iv. 12—13.
|| Rev. iii. 1 & iv. 5.   § Rev. v. 5 & iii. 7.   ¶ Psa. ciii. 20.
** Rev. vii. 17.

Ten thousand times ten thousand then,
Thousands of thousands those again!
No man can tell their number now,
Or their true number find and show!

They praise the Lamb who once was slain,
Whose regal right it is to reign,
Ascribe to Him all power and might,
Wisdom and riches as His right.

Honor and glory to Him give,
And He all blessing doth receive,
For Him they worship and adore,
Who lives and reigns for evermore.

THE SONG OF ANGELS AND MEN!
Rev. v. 11—13.   S's.

255. Worthy is the Lamb that was slain,
To reign in His Kingdom again,
To receive as in His own right,
All wisdom and riches and might.

Let honor and glory be giv'n,
And blessing in earth and in heav'n,
Him all praises and worship we'll give,
Who for ever and ever will live.

"THE SEVENTH SEAL!"
Rev. viii. 1—5.   S's & 7's.

256. When the seventh seal is broken,
   As the Spirit long hath shown,
Great events which God hath spoken
   Will be manifest and known.

Voices from Himself revealing,
   Changes taking place on earth,
With His *mystic* thunders pealing,
   And His light'nings flashing forth!

Babel will be overtaken,
    And the world itself will quail
Greatly by an earthquake shaken,
    In the last great storm of hail! *

Now their heav'ns are seen receding,
    As their mountains break and flee,
All earth's stately glory fading,
    Disappearing with its sea! †

Many from their slumbers waking,
    Unprepar'd to stand the test,
All their idols are forsaking,
    And are earnest seeking rest.

Then the Lord will grant His blessing,
    As He never did before,
And His saints the fruits possessing,
    Former troubles are no more!

THE FIERY MOUNTAIN!
Rev. viii. 8, 9.   7's & 6's.

257. Behold a mountain burning,
    Into the sea is hurl'd,
To blood its waters turning,
    Those waters are the world. ‡

The mountain is a kingdom! ||
    As prophecy will show,
Its Antichrist's dominion,
    And His religion too!

As its waters then were turned,
    Or curdled into blood,
And as this great mountain burned,
    May this be understood:

Its fire is the fire of wrath,
    Which is the fire of hell!
And the blood the sign of death, §
    As truth will plainly tell!

* Rev. xvi. 21.   † Rev. xxi. 1.
‡ Rev. xvii. 15. || Jer. li. 25.   § Rev. xvi. 3.

So men spiritually died;
　　Far as its wrath was felt,
It hardening power applied,
　　And in destruction dealt.

And so there they have no rest,
　　Neither by day nor night,
Of evil they are possest,
　　And have no other right.

And unless they should repent,
　　And are through Christ forgiv'n,
They will evermore lament
　　Their loss of life and heav'n.

THE ANGEL'S PROCLAMATION!
Rev. x. 1—7.   L.M.

258. A mighty Angel cometh down
　　From high heaven unto the earth,
That He His purpose may make known,
　　And sound His proclamation forth;

His person, covered with a cloud,
　　Is hidden from all mortal sight:
This does His blazing glory shroud,
　　And His insufferable light!

A *rainbow* circles o'er His head,
　　Which must an holy awe inspire;
And wheresoever He doth tread,
　　His feet are like pillars of fire!

His face, which shineth as the sun,
　　Doth plainly unto us reveal
That He is the Almighty One
　　Who maketh known His sovereign will!

With one foot standing on the sea,
　　The other resting on the land,
He lifts His hand in majesty,
　　The deeper silence to command;

His hand He lifts to heaven, and swears
  By Him who lives for evermore;
So that the truth which He declares
  It never can be made more sure;

That, when the *seventh trump* shall sound,
  For things long hidden and concealed,
Time will no longer then be found,
  But His mystery stand revealed!

THE "TWO WITNESSES!"
Rev. xi. 3—4; Zech. iv. 3; xi., 14.

259. The living witnesses for God
  Who have for many years
The path of tribulation trod
  In this dark vale of tears,

They prophesy, the Spirit says,
  As they have a command,
For twelve hundred and sixty days,
  And, clothed in sackcloth stand!

These are the two anointed ones,
  Standing before the Lord!
And, as His consecrated sons,*
  Preach the life-giving Word!

These are the two green olive trees,
  Bearing rich fruit to God!
Two golden candlesticks are these,
  Shedding their *light* abroad!

Of Jewish and of Christian might,
  We see those Churches stand;
One on the left, one on the right,
  And each has His command!

For twelve hundred and sixty years
  Their prophecies are heard;
And after that the Lord appears,
  To give them their reward.

* Zech. iv. 14. See margin.

When He is heard, and He alone,
  Grace greater than before
Shall then unite them both as one,
  To serve Him evermore!

THE SEVENTH TRUMPET!
ITS FIRST SPECIAL APPLICATION.

Rev. xi. 15.   C. M.

260. Attend the seventh trumpet's sound,
  While Christ His pow'r reveals;
The mystery now seal'd is found,
  But He removes the seals!

Yea, hear the seventh trumpet's voice,
  Whoe'er the Spirit hears;
Ye virgin waiting souls rejoice,
  The Bridegroom now appears!

The mystery is plainly seen
  By His revealing light,
Which hidden hath for ages been,
  And covered with the night;

'Tis Christ in you, your living Lord,
  Your hope of glory too,
The wonderful creating Word,
  Who maketh all things new!

THE SEVENTH TRUMPET!
ITS SECOND GENERAL MEANING.

Rev. xi. 15—19.   7's & 6's.

261. Hark, the seventh trumpet sounds!
  The mystery of old;
Light and knowledge now abounds,
  By prophecy foretold.

Now the kingdoms are become
    The kingdoms of the Lord ;
Now He doth His power assume,
    His people to reward !

Now the veil is fully rent,
    And the blest sight is giv'n
The ark of His testament,
    In the temple of heav'n !

Voices now are heard on earth,
    And lightnings shine abroad,
Awful thunders issue forth,
    And an earthquake, from God !

Th' earthquake follow'd is by hail
    Both terrible and great ;
All His enemies shall wail
    The punishment of it.

But His saints the triumph sing,
    Delivered from their fears :
They shall live with Christ their King,
    And reign a thousand years !

SYMBOLICAL REPRESENTATIONS OF THE TRUE CHURCH, AND HER MIGHTY ENEMY THE GREAT RED DRAGON !

Rev. xii. 1—6.   J.M.

262. Behold a wonder seen in heav'n,
    The goodly sight to all is giv'n
    Who are ingathered from the night,
    And now enlightened with true light :

A woman clothèd with the sun,
    Twelve brilliant stars compose her crown :
    Under her feet appears the moon,
    While all above is sacred noon !

The woman, travailing in birth,
Brought forth a Son to rule the earth,
Who did His name and pow'r express
By works of truth and righteousness!

Another wonder seen in heav'n,
A great red Dragon, who had striv'n
Hard to destroy the woman's Child
As soon as born, though undefil'd.

The Dragon he had seven heads,
And seven crowns them overspreads.
While from his heads proceed ten horns,
Both crowns and grandeur them adorns.

Now the man-child ascends to God,
To rule the earth with iron rod;
And the grieved woman, in distress,
Flies far into the wilderness!

For times a time and half a time
She's nourish'd in a des'late clime;
There against her the Dragon stood,
Who strove to drown her with his flood.

Still preservation she obtains
From Him who now in glory reigns;
By whom her restoration's sure
To greater glory than before!

THE GREAT RED DRAGON!

Rev. xii. 3, 4.

263. Seven heads the Dragon has,
    And ten horns upon his heads,
  Terrible at first he was
    Who the "whore" of nations leads.

Him she worships and adores,
  Who hath led her from the light:
Who his government secures
  Under cover of the night!

See the monster, bloody red,
  Fill'd with savage joy and mirth,
Now his tail the *stars* hath led,
  And a *third* cast on the earth!

He hath fill'd her golden cup,
  Which she holds to great and small;
And the beast he hath rais'd up *
  In dominion over all!

All the world worship the Beast,
  With the Dragon who did raise,
From the greatest to the least,
  And his pow'r and greatness praise.

None but saints the vict'ry know †
  O'er his number, mark, and name;
All the rest unto him bow,
  And extol the Dragon's fame.

THE CHURCH COMING UP FROM THE WILDERNESS, LEANING ON THE ARM OF HER BELOVED, AFTER AN ISOLATED SOJOURN OF 1,260 YEARS!

Rev. xii. 6—14; Cant. viii. 5 & vi. 10.   C. M.

264. Who cometh from the wilderness,
      Arrayed in pow'r and might,
    In glorious truth and righteousness,
      And everlasting light.

  Whose arm it is all pow'rful,
    To save and to destroy,
  Whose name it is most wonderful,
    The highest of the high!

* Rev. xiii. 2—8.   † Rev. xvii. 8 & xv. 2.

And who is it that is leaning
  On her beloved now?
See her face with conquest beaming,
  Her garments white as snow!

With the holy oil anointed,
  And rich in its perfumes,
Her redemption, long appointed,
  With joy and gladness comes!

Clothèd with her sun's adorning,
  And fair as the clear moon,
Lo! she shineth as the morning,
  Or as the day at noon!

She cometh from the wilderness,
  Her last and long abode.
Bedeckèd in her bridal dress,
  The living church of God!

THE BEAST REPRESENTING THE FOURTH UNIVERSAL MONARCHY!

Rev. xiii. 1—9. 8's & 7's.

265. See the monster Beast uprising
  From the waters of the sea;
He is wondrous and surprising
  Unto all, both bond and free.

He is like a leopard: fleetly!
  Terrible his feet as bears'!
His a lion's mouth completely,
  Which the prey in pieces tears!

Seven heads he doth discover,
  And ten horns upon his heads;
Golden crowns his horns to cover:
  Thus his fame and greatness spreads.

Lo! the Dragon gives his power.
  And his seat unto the Beast:
As his God and benefactor,
  With his government invest!

Thus he ruleth for the Dragon,
  Nor his blasphemies withdraws;
Wide increasing his dominion
  By his anti-Christian laws.

Forty-and-two months appointed
  To continue in renown,
Then his kingdom is disjointed,
  And his reign is overthrown!

In his times, it's truly spoken,
  All the world shall worship him;
This to saints is a sure token,
  Who are suff'ring under him.

You can read this dark relation
  By the spirit of the Lord;
Though you are in lowly station,
  Waiting vict'ry by His Word.

THE TWO HORNED BEAST!
Rev. xiii. 11.   C. M.

266. Behold the beast that's like a Lamb,
  Arising from the earth;
He cometh up in Jesus' name,
  Without a claim by birth!

Two noted horns are on his head,
  From these his greatness springs;
By these his worldly pow'r hath spread,
  And rule in sacred things!

He claims a government divine,
  Likewise an earthly throne,
And in both characters doth shine
  As none besides have done.

His eyes are like sharp human eyes;
  He speaketh of high things;
And trading in proud heresies
  To him all treasure brings!

The hand of truth his portrait paints,
  And he is clearly seen
A persecutor of the saints,
  As he hath always been!

For twelve hundred and sixty years
  He will his arts employ,
And then the *ten*-horn'd pow'r appears
  Which will his reign destroy.

And soon his worldly pomp will cease,
  Which many did befriend,
And his spiritual pow'r decrease,
  Till both shall have an end.

THE TWO HORNED BEAST!

Rev. xiii. 11—18.

267. He who cometh like a Lamb,
  Yet as a Dragon speaks;
He who comes in Jesus' name,
  Yet his own glory seeks.

As a Lamb, gentle, and meek,
  His profession accords;
As a Dragon he doth speak
  With most deceitful words.

His two horns he wears before,
  Which on his head are seen,
Are the symbols of his power,
  As they have always been!

Thus he claims a pow'r divine
    Unto the church below;
Does with this a rule combine,
    Whence earthly treasures flow!

By false signs and wonders great*
    He does the world deceive;
And he takes the highest seat
    That wealth and greatness give!

Many unto him submit,
    And fear his shaken rod,
Who does in the temple sit
    As if he were a God!

Yet his end approaches fast,
    When all he now appears
Will be written of as past,
    Or things of bygone years.

When the Son of God shall come,
    And angels him attend,
Then his glory will consume,
    And have a final end.

THE MYSTICAL NUMBER 666!

Rev. xiii. 18.

268. Lo! "Here is wisdom" saith the Lord,
    Which demonstration will afford
    Unto the understanding mind,
    When it the numbered beast shall find!

His is the number of a man,
    Now search this problem all who can;
    On each the number truth doth fix
    As six hundred and sixty-six!

* 2 Thes. ii. 3—12.

This earthly number marks the bound
To all the wisdom men have found;
And let the boasted powers of man
Surpass this number if they can!

The Spirit doth man's number fix,
And limit it to 6—6—6!
But him as man no power hath given
To reach and grasp the number 7!

THE ANGEL'S MESSAGE!
Rev. xiv. 6, 7.
7's.

269. Now the gospel word is giv'n,
    Which the Angel doth proclaim:
Worship ye the God of heav'n,
    And give glory unto Him.

He who made all worlds above,
    And created all below;
He whose pow'r doth o'er all move,
    And to whom all things must bow.

For His *hour* of judgment's come,
    And His day of wrath confest,
Which false systems will consume,
    From the east unto the west.

Then all men shall know the Lord,
    And His will on earth be done:
Him shall serve with one accord,
    And shall worship Him alone!

THE ANGEL'S PROCLAMATION!
Rev. xiv. 6, 7.
7's.

270. Listen to the voice of God,
    Hear the message of the Lord,
Which He now proclaims aloud
    By the Gospel of His Word.*

* John i. 1; Pet. i. 25.

Fear and serve ye Me alone,
   And give glory to My name ;
I am the Almighty One,
   And from Me all being came!

I alone have made all things,
   And from Me they had their birth ;
I, who am the King of kings,
   In the heavens and the earth!

For My *hour* of judgment's come,
   Now Great Babylon shall fall :
She must in My fire consume,
   And be found no more at all.

"A VOICE FROM HEAVEN."

Rev. xiv. 13.   C. M.

271. A voice which spake from heav'n is heard,
   Saying the dead are blest
Who henceforth shall die in the Lord,
   For they shall ever rest.

From all their labors, toils, and pains,
   Sweet rest to them is giv'n :
The rest which evermore remains
   As their reward in heav'n!

Their souls in purity and peace,
   Without a cloud above,
Enjoy the smiles of Jesus' face
   And riches of His love!

There in the realms of glory bright,
   Their new unfading home,
They bask in pleasures of delight,
   With always joys to come!

THE PEACEFUL AND HAPPY DEATH OF BELIEVERS.

Rev. xiv. 13. 11's.

How glorious th' prospect of Saints at their death,
   Not with terrific visions or feelings opprest;
But, cheerfully yielding their spir't and breath,
   Are instantly borne to the home of the blest.

It is true for a while darkness may assail,
   And so be the cause of some gathering fears;
But that they should not in their confidence fail,
   Jesus, the good Shepherd, to help them appears.

Then their doubts are all fled and their troubles all gone,
   When th' molesting darkness is chang'd into light;
As their sun in its holy meridian shone,
   Confirming and turning their faith into sight!

Angels do th' honor to attend on their bed,
   Receiving their peaceful commission from God;
Lo! a pause, and th' immortal spirit is fled
   To th' mansion prepared for its future abode.

Lo! an entrance to glory is ministered then,
   The kingdom which standeth for ever above:
Where its triumphs in unceasing pleasures are seen,
   Combined with the tokens of permanent love.

Their spirits are landed on Canaan's bright shore,
   Secure from the hatred and malice of foes;
They rest where their weeping and pain are no more,
   In th' land of a sweet everlasting repose.

SAINTS IN GLORY!

Rev. xiv. 13.   S. M.

273. How happy are the saints
    That rest secure in heav'n,
No language speaks nor fancy paints
    The grace and glory giv'n!

    On that celestial shore
    Where truth for ever reigns,
Where toils and troubles are no more,
    And blissful peace remains.

    They dwell before His face,
    The presence of the Lord,
Where streams of overpow'ring grace
    Triumphant joys afford!

    How ravishing the sight,
    It doth our faith transcend,
Where glory in perfection's height
    Will never know an end!

MEMORIALS OF THE DEAD!

Rev. xiv. 13.   L. M.

274. Sweet is th' memory of the dead,
Whose spirits live with Christ their head:
Who, saved by grace, through faith alone,
Are from this world of trouble gone.

Sweet is th' memory of their lives,
And one instruction thence derives,
Pure was the air they seemed to breathe,
Searching their words, and calm their death.

Sweet is th' memory of their end,
Which angel messengers attend,
Their holy escort guide and guard
To mansions which the Lord prepar'd.

Sweet is th' memory of their grace,
Dwelling before the Saviour's face,
Like stars' and suns' created light,
Shining in glory ever bright!

THE GATHERING HOME OF THE PEOPLE OF GOD! AND THE DESTRUCTION OF ANTICHRIST AND HIS PEOPLE.

Rev. xiv. 14—20. L. M.

275. An angel sits on a *white* cloud,
Which does His blazing glory shroud;
Wears on His head a crown of gold,
And owns a name that is untold. *

This mighty Angel, understand,
Holds a sharp sickle in His hand,
Who, when His *ensigns* are unfurl'd,
Will reap the harvest of the world!

A second angel now appears,
A sickle with strong arm he bears;
And then a third in wrathful ire,
Who holds dominion over fire.

By Him is the commission giv'n,
Unto the angel sent from heav'n,
To gather clusters of the vine,
Which hath assumed a name divine!

The angel thrusts his sickle forth,
And reaps the vintage of the earth,
In the great press it then is trod,
The winepress of the wrath of God.

The issue is a stream of blood,
Which, like an overflowing flood,
Will show the vengeance sin hath stor'd,
And the just judgment of the Lord.

* Rev. xix. 12.

PRAISE BY THE SAINTS IN GLORY.
Rev. xv. 2—4. C. M.

276. Great and marvellous are Thy acts,
  Most high and mighty God,
The wonders which Thy arm transacts
  With an uplifted rod.

What glor'ous deeds Thy hand displays,
  Confin'd by no restraints,
How just and true are all Thy ways
  Almighty King of saints!

Who would not fear Thy dreadful name,
  And humbly bow the knee;
All nations hearing of Thy fame
  Shall come and worship Thee.

For Thy just judgments on the earth
  Now manifested are,
And her enlighten'd tribes go forth,
  Thy praises to declare!

THE SONG OF MOSES AND THE LAMB.
Rev. xv. 3. C. M.

277. Arise, my soul, with all thy pow'rs
  List to th' angelic throng,
Who gladden heav'n's immortal bow'rs
  With the immortal song:

The Song of Moses and the Lamb,
  The justice, truth, and grace,
Comprising all in Jesus' name,
  The glory of the place.

The law which God by Moses gave,
  They sing with grave accord;
But the almighty pow'r to save,
  That dwells in Christ the Lord,

Inflames their minds with burning love,
And wafts their strains along:
To Him the chants of praises move,
And well completes the song!

THE SONG OF MOSES AND THE LAMB
Rev. xv. 3.
C. M.

278. Now we arise, and sing the Song
Of Moses and the Lamb:
Salvation doth to Christ belong,
And glory to His name!

By Moses led, Israel went out
From under Pharaoh's hand;
They trode the wilderness about,
Yet reached not Canaan's land.

But, Jesus, Captain of the host,*
Whom Joshua, Lord confest,
Led beyond Jordan and its coast
Into the promised rest!

Thus, while we Moses' vict'ries sing,
And learn the legal state,
We're pointed unto Israel's King,
Whose triumphs are complete.

Salvation, the Mosaic theme,†
The burden of the song,
Salvation to the Saviour's name!
Who does the theme prolong.

Salvation by His conqu'ring sword!
Salvation high in fame!
Salvation to our Sov'reign Lord!
Salvation to the Lamb!

* Josh. v. 13—15. † Ex xv. 1, 2.

THE VIALS OF WRATH.

Rev. xvi. 1—12.   7's & 6's.

279. The first vial, when pour'd forth,
    Fretted on all a sore
Who worshipp'd the Beast on earth,
    His *mark* or *image* bore!

The vial pour'd on the sea,
    Its waters turned to blood;
By the waters of the sea,
    Peoples are understood.*

On its tributary streams,
    Where the next vial fell,
By its burning wrath it seems
    They blood became as well.

Then the fourth it fell upon,
    Seething with wrathful ire,
The dark world's mystical sun,
    Which scorch'd men with his fire!

And the next pour'd on the seat,
    Or where the Beast doth reign;
There the darkness was so great,
    They gnaw'd their tongues for pain!

That which on the river fell,
    The Euphrates by name,
There its scorching heat would tell
    By drying up the same.

Ev'ry vial fill'd with wrath,
    Wherever it may fall,
Spiritually worketh death,
    Which reacheth unto all.

All these wrathful plagues are hurl'd
    As punishment for sins,
On the Antichristian world,†
    Or where the Woman reigns!

* Rev. xvii. 15.   † Rev. xvii. 18.

THE VIALS OF WRATH.

Rev. xvi. 1—12, 17. L. M.

280. The vial pour'd in judgment forth,
    On men became a noisome sore;
Who worshippèd the Beast on earth,
    His *image* or his *mark* who bore!

The second, pour'd upon the sea,
    By sea nations are understood,
When death followed immediately,
    Its waters being turned to blood.

The third upon the rivers fell,
    Whose waters run into the sea,
When they were turned to blood as well,
    A judgment for their cruelty!

The fourth vial fell on the sun,
    Kindling afresh his wrathful ire,
Whereby all those he shone upon
    Were burned or scorchèd with his fire!

The fifth vial fell on the seat,
    Or where the Beast doth sit and reign;
The darkness then became so great,
    His creatures knaw'd their tongues for pain!

The sixth on the great river fell,
    The river Euphrates by name,
Whereon its fiery heat would tell,
    By wholly drying up the same.

The last vial fell on the air,
    When the great mystery is done;
Voices from God will then declare
    All things to each elected one!

THE LAST VIAL!

Rev. xvi. 17—21.   7's.

281. Lo! the seventh angel pours
    His dread vial forth abroad,
On the *air* the wrath he show'rs,
    With a trumpet's voice from God!

Heav'nly voices now respond,
    Lightnings from on high are hurl'd,
Awful thunders roll around,
    And an earthquake shakes the world!

The great city doth divide,
    In three parts it now is found;
Cities of the earth, beside,
    Reel and totter to the ground.

Heavy *hail* succeedeth all,
    And the plague of it is great:
Out of heav'n the showers fall,
    Stones about a *talent* weight!

Now great Babylon hath sunk,
    Judgment meted her is sore:
She that made all nations drunk,
    Drinks to fall and rise no more.

She hath met her heavy doom,
    All the wicked with her share;
Sinners find a day of gloom,
    While the saints triumphant are.

Now they shall His honors sing,
    Who hath got them high renown;
Who on earth shall reign as King,
    And for ever wear the crown!

"MYSTERY! BABYLON THE GREAT! THE MOTHER OF HARLOTS! AND ABOMINATIONS OF THE EARTH!"

Rev. xvii. & xviii. chs.   L. M.

282. Mystery, Babylon the great,
　　The mother of all harlots she,
　The painted "Whore," whose colors cheat,
　　And draw the world to infamy.

　The cup she in her hand doth hold *
　　Of fornicating wine is full :
　The wine of wrath, though served in gold,
　　And proves a poison to the soul!

　She on the Beast hath fix'd her seat,
　　Which in the wilderness we see :
　The reigning Beast, his pow'r is great,
　　Whose *horns* will her destroyers be!

　But oh, how marvellous it is,
　　That those to whom she holds her cup,
　Should first supply the "Whore" with this,
　　And from their given treasure sup!

　No wonder that their worship's paid
　　Unto th' Beast which carrieth her,
　Their off'rings at her feet are laid,
　　And she is their interpreter!

　Behold her drunk with blood of saints,
　　And blood of martyrs of the Lord :
　He'll soon avenge their long complaints,
　　And His almighty help afford.

　For half a time, a time, and times,
　　Must she continue in her pow'r,
　And then be punish'd for her crimes,
　　Yea, be destroyed in one *hour!*

* Rev. xvii. 4.

Like a great stone flung in the sea,
  Which plunges swift, to rise no more,
So shall at last her downfall be,
  Her judgment is decreed and sure!

The Angel of the Lord descends,*
  In might and majesty array'd;
Glory and terror him attends,
  While a bright *bow* surrounds his head.

He speaks the triumph all abroad,
  His people listen to His voice;
It is the Lord their Saviour, God,
  They worship Him, give thanks, rejoice.

Fear God, and glory give to Him,†
  And worship Him, who made the earth,
And heav'n, with all that live in them,
  And gave the seas and fountains birth.

For the *hour* of His judgment's come,
  Let kings and princes hear His words;
He'll now His reigning power assume,
  And hence their kingdoms are the Lord's!

THE FALL OF BABYLON!
Rev. xviii. 1—19.   L. M.

283. A mighty Angel now descends,
  He cometh with all honors crown'd,
Both light and glory him attends,
  And shine the spacious earth around.

Of Babylon the great he cries,
  She's *fallen, fallen*, he repeats!
And swift the proclamation flies
  Through her proud city and her streets.

* Rev. x. 1 and xviii. 1.   † Rev. xiv. 6, 7.

Astonishment and dread surprise
  Fill all her citizens with gloom,
And fearful consternations rise,
  Which but bespeak her sudden doom!

Merchants and great men of the earth,
  Who traded in her merchandise,
Behold her judgments issue forth,
  And vent their griefs with mournful cries.

All that in ships of trading sail
  To this great "Queen of kingdoms'" home,
Over her burning weep and wail,
  For in *one hour* her judgment's come!

All that before her favors sought,
  Lament and wail over her fate:
For in *one hour* all's come to nought,
  And she is made most desolate!

And from her great and grievous fall,
  No hand or pow'r can her release;
Her riches, pomp, and glory shall
  From thenceforth and for ever cease.

ANGELS AND SAINTS INVITED TO REJOICE OVER THE FALL OF BABYLON!

Rev. xviii. 20. S. M.

284. Great Babylon shall fall,
  And never rise again,
Be changed her pomp and glory shall,
  To misery and pain.

  Over her fallen state,
    The heav'ns aloud rejoice,
  Prophets and saints their songs unite,
    With an exalted voice.

The triumphs of that hour
Shall ne'er forgotten be,
Nor grateful praises cease to pour
To all eternity.

THEY UNITE IN PRAISES TO GOD.
Rev. xix. 1—6. C. M.

285. All heav'n and earth their voices raise,
And Hallelujahs sing,
Aspiring in triumphant praise
To heav'n's eternal King.

Worthy the Lord omnipotent,
All glory to receive,
Who should immortal songs be spent,
Doth still for ever live.

THE TRIUMPHANT CELEBRATION OF THE FALL OF BABYLON BY (ANGELS AND) THE PEOPLE OF GOD!
Rev. xix. 1—6. L. M.

286. Loud Hallelujah's now we sing,
Unto the high eternal King,
Salvation, glory, honor, power,
To th' Lord our God for evermore!

By Him the "Whore" of nations fell,
And sunk in darkness down to dwell;
He hath avenged His servants' blood,
By His just judgments like a flood.

The great Omnipotent now reigns,
His kingdom over all maintains,
Proclaims His sov'reign right abroad,
The holy, true, and righteous God.

Now heav'n and earth aspire to raise
Their voices in triumphant praise,
Vast multitudes, in songs record
Loud Hallelujahs to the Lord!

Loud Hallelujahs now we sing,
Unto the high eternal King,
Salvation, glory, honor, power,
To th' Lord our God for evermore!

CHRIST DESTROYING THE ENEMIES OF HIS CHURCH AND PEOPLE.

Rev. xix. 11—16.   L. M.

287. His name is call'd the Word of God;
Come, see His vesture dipped in blood,
For when He hath the winepress trod,
Blood will stream from it like a flood.*

The winepress of God's mighty wrath,
Trodden without our Zion's walls,
The vintage which He cursèd hath,
On it His foot of vengeance falls!

Her grapes are only grapes of gall,
Her clusters, bitter to the soul;
And so will taste unto them all,
Long as eternal ages roll.

The antichristian vintage this,
Which will be trodden by the Lord;
His wrath, which manifested is,
On that devoted Church is pour'd!

Then let the angel's warning voice †
Be heard, before she disappear;
For then His vineyard shall rejoice,
Who now the many crowns doth wear!

* Rev. xiv. 18—20.   † Rev. xiv. 6, 7; xviii. 4.

THE WORD OF GOD TREADING THE WINEPRESS OF HIS WRATH.

Rev. xix. 13—15. L. M.

288. His name is call'd the Word of God,
   He, who the winepress treads alone,
And who will publish all abroad,
   The mighty work which He hath done.

The winepress of God's wrath He treads,
   Fill'd with the clusters of the vine,
Which on the earth now grows and spreads,
   And with a name that seems divine!

It trodden is without the walls*
   Of God's true city here below;
And the press'd blood which from it falls,
   Will like a stream or river flow.

Then will He plant His noble vine,
   One that is wholly a right seed,
Which will produce the fruits divine,
   And earth His vineyard be indeed.

For He will keep it night and day,†
   Will ev'ry moment water it;
And, pruned and dressed in His own way.
   He will accept the fruit of it.

Thus the whole vineyard is the Lord's,
   And the true Church His goodly plant:
He His own sap of life affords,
   Nor will it His protection want.

A VOICE FROM THE THRONE.

Rev. xix. 5, 6.‡ L. M.

289. From the high throne of God in heav'n,
By a strong voice command is giv'n,
That He should then be prais'd by all
That fear and serve Him, great and small.

* Rev. xiv. 19, 20.   † Isa. xxvii. 2, 3.
‡ Rev v. 11—13 and vii. 9—12.

Ten thousand times ten thousand now,
And thousands of those thousands show
A number so immensely great,
No man could number and repeat!

All with one mind their voices raise,
And the Almighty Saviour praise;
In holy worship Him adore,
Who lives and reigns for evermore.

THE TRIUMPH OF THE CHURCH OF GOD OVER HER ENEMIES.
Rev. xix. 1—6.* C.M.

290. A song of triumph now is heard,
  In the true Church of God;
And highest praise for Him prepar'd
  Who hath the winepress trod.

In the wrath's winepress He alone
  Hath trodden down the "whore:"
Her power is now for ever gone,
  And will be known no more.

She hath a persecutor been,
  A slayer of the good;
And in His day of wrath is seen,
  Th' avenging of their blood!

Then let the sound of vict'ry ring
  Through the whole earth abroad;
And all His favor'd people bring
  Their offerings to God.

THE SAINTS' VICTORY.
Rev. xix. 11—16. 7's.

291. Glory in the Lord your God,
  Glory in His holy name,
By whose pow'r alone ye stood,
  By whose strength ye overcame;

* Isa. lxiii. 1—6; Rev. xix. 13—16; and xiv. 18—20.

Though your foes as waters were,
    Gather'd round to make you fall,
God himself was with you there,
    And responded to your call.

For your enemies were great,
    You as nothing in their sight,
Yet you gave them a defeat,
    And the aliens put to flight.

It was then your King went forth,
    Arm'd with sword, on His white horse,
'Gainst destroyers of the earth,
    To o'erturn their sinful course.

Thus He wars against the Beast,*
    Who with the false prophet join'd,
Bring their armies to the test,
    And a vale of slaughter find!

Then He will the Dragon bind †
    With His chain of matchless power,
Till disabled and confin'd
    For a thousand years secure!

When the thousand are fulfill'd,
    Satan must be loos'd again;
Train new armies for the field,
    Which by fire alone are slain.

Thus the saints the vict'ry have
    Not by carnal sword or spear,
God almighty does them save,
    Their great Leader in the war!

THE ALMIGHTY RULER OF THE UNIVERSE!
Rev. xix. 11—16.   L. M.

292. The King of kings and Lord of lords
    Proclaims His titles from on high,
And His own sovereignty records
    Upon His vesture, and His thigh!

* Rev. xix. 19—21.   † Rev. xx. 1—3, 7—9.

His name is call'd the Word of God:
   The keys of hell and death He hath;
He rules His foes with iron rod,
   And treads the wine-press of His wrath.

Let nations own His regal fame,
   Who bears the all-avenging sword,
And bow before His dreadful name,
   Obedient to His sov'reign word.

The time is come when He must reign,
   And make His enemies submit,
Till sole dominion He obtain,
   And all things put beneath His feet!

THE GREAT BATTLE BETWEEN HEAVEN AND EARTH.

Rev. xix. 11—21.   8's & 7's.

293. When John, who in a heav'nly vision
   Saw the Saviour's army move,
Light and glory did emblazon
   All His shining host above.

All were on white horses seated,
   Clothed in garments pure and white,
For the battle all outfitted,
   Arms and armour for the fight.

At His word they all move forward,
   With their streaming banners bright,
He, their Captain, leads them onward,
   That they may His battles fight!

See Him as a mighty warrior,
   On His milk-white charger sit,
Crown'd with many crowns, as Conqu'ror;
   He will make His foes submit.

See the Beast his forces gather
  For the fight, with one accord,
But his power and glory wither
  In the presence of the Lord!

All their ranks are slain or scatter'd
  By the sword out of His mouth;
And their arms and armour shatter'd
  By His word of potent truth.

The Beast's numerous forces kill'd,
  Multitudes of dead afford:
And the fowls of heaven are fill'd
  At the supper of the Lord!

THE FINAL CONQUEST!
Rev. xix. 11—21.

294. He who wears many crowns on high,
  His sole prerogatives records
On His vesture, and on His thigh,
  As King of kings and Lord of lords.

He hath a hidden secret name;
  He is the just, the holy God;
His eyes are as the burning flame,
  Who rules His foes with iron rod.

He will His mighty acts record,
  Who maketh war in righteousness;
And in the slaughter by His sword
  He will men's wickedness repress.

The rebels now against Him fight,
  Yet cannot in His presence stand;
They quail before His warlike might,
  And fall by His destroying hand.

The sounds of victory are heard
  Where'er the conflict has begun;
And praise and worship are prepar'd
  For Him who hath the battle won.

When He His enemies hath slain,
　His proclamation will go forth,
Which will inaugurate His reign,
　His final government on earth!

THE PROCLAMATION OF AN ANGEL STANDING IN THE SUN!

Rev. xix. 17—21.　　　L. M.

295. An angel standing in the sun,
　　Crieth to all the fowls of heav'n—
Gather yourselves, nor seek to shun
　　The invitation which is giv'n.

To flying fowls he cries aloud,
　　And doth them now together call
Unto the supper of their God,
　　That they may eat the flesh of all—

Horses, and those that on them sit,
　　And small and great, and free and bond,
The Beast with all his armies met,
　　Which will be smitten on the ground.

Lo! all their fighting ones are slain,
　　By the destroying sword of Him
Who will His righteous cause maintain,
　　And scatter all the spoils to them.

For all the fowls of heav'n are spread
　　Upon the slaughter'd all around:
Feasting upon the silent dead,
　　Till satiated they are found.

Let those who witness this declare
　　The dread of His avenging sword;
And those that read the *signs* beware,
　　That they are faithful to the Lord.

THE ANGELS' PROCLAMATION AND ITS RESULTS.

Rev. xix. 17, 21.   L. M.

296. An angel standing in the sun,
A glor'ous, highly-favor'd one:
An angel great in pow'r and might,
Crieth from his exalted height,

To all the feather'd fowls that fly,
In open air or open sky,
Wherever now scatter'd abroad,
Come to the supper of our God:

That ye may eat the flesh of kings,
And flesh of armies the Beast brings,
With all his heroes far and nigh,
To fight against the Lord most High!

Heav'n's mighty warrior behold,
The *ensigns* of His pow'r unfold,
While He His sov'reignty records,
As King of kings and Lord of lords.

He leads His chosen army on,
In dazzling splendor, like the sun;
And His *first ensign* marks His fame,
A *Lion* this, of awful name!

At the dread sight His foes will quail,
And all their arms and armour fail;
For, to the Beast the battle's lost,
The sword hath smitten all his host.

The Armageddon where they fell,[*]
We multitudes of corpses tell;
There all the fowls of heav'n are spread,
Feasting upon the silent dead.

[*] Rev. xvi. 12—16.

His *second ensign* now appears,
A mild and *gentle Lamb* it bears;
And now His reign of peace begins,
And over all the earth He reigns!

THE LAST JUDGMENT.

Rev. xx. 11—15.

297. Hark! a voice the trumpet soundeth,
　　Swift the dreadful summons flies;
It is the Judge; behold! He cometh,
　　With His numberless allies.
See Him coming, with His chariot, from the skies.

See Him in the clouds appearing,
　　With immortal honors crown'd;
And the light, which He is wearing
　　As a garment, clothe him round;
Bliss and terror, deck the scene with awe profound.

Thunders roar without cessations,
　　Lightnings flash around the sphere,
Discovering its deep foundations,
　　Burning with devouring fire;
The heav'ns departing, and as melting wax expire.*

See the Judge, with flames to guard Him,
　　Seated on His great white throne;
Thousands, thousands stand before Him,
　　To receive as they have done,
By the hand of God, in righteousness alone.

See the open books, exposing
　　All their words, and all their acts;
And each countenance disclosing
　　Attestations of the facts;
Judgment proceeds, and its solemn work transacts.

* 2 Pet. iii 10.

Sinners in confusions hurry,
  Sink in mis'ry at His word ;
While the saints, in shining glory,
  Join in praises to the Lord ;
Endless ages, their triumphant joys record.

THE HOLY CITY, THE NEW JERUSALEM !

Rev. xxi. 9—27.   C. M.

298. Zion, the city of our God,
  How glor'ous to behold,
Her gates are pearls most richly hued,
  Her streets are purest gold.

Her foundations are strongly laid,
  With massive stones of light ;
Her wall, too, is of jasper made
  Exquisite to the sight.

On her twelve gates are Israel's tribes,
  By name upon record ;
On her foundations are inscribed
  The apostles of the Lord !

The city is a perfect square :
  As the height of her frame,
With length and breadth, quite equal are,
  All measuring the same !

This is the new Jerusalem, *
  No outward temple there :
God and the Lamb are light to them
  Who in her glories share.

And in it shall the nations dwell,
  Saved by her light and power,
And their immortal pleasures tell,
  Thenceforth and evermore.

* Heb. xii. 22—24 ; Gal. iv. 26.

"THERE SHALL BE NO NIGHT THERE!"

Rev. xxii. 5. L.M.

299. In the glad City of the Lord,
    It is all day, there is no night,
God, by His presence, doth afford,
    And is her everlasting light.

He is her centre and her sun,
    Fountain and source of all her bliss,
There pure immortal joys are known,
    And holy praises never cease.

There will the saints in glory dwell,
    Saved by His matchless love and power,
Her unknown wonders see and tell,
    And reign in life for evermore!

TRUE CHRISTIANS ARE BLESSED.

Rev. xxii. 14. C.M.

300. Blessed are those that do obey.
    And truly serve the Lord,
His special acts of goodness they
    Are favored to record.

Such have a right unto the tree,
    Which fruit immortal bears:
They daily learn, and taste, and see,
    How vast its life appears!

They know the gate, and enter in
    The City of the Lord,
Where all is light and joy within,
    And constant praise is heard!

None but God's children there may dwell,
   And it is those alone
Can its exceeding riches tell,
   On whom its light hath shone.

UNIVERSAL INVITATION.

Rev. xxii. 17.

301. The Spirit and the Bride say come,
   And let him come that is athirst,
Whoever will may return home
   And know the saving pow'r of Christ!

Let him that heareth this say come,
   Unto lost sinners ev'rywhere,
Nor through deception dare presume
   Another doctrine to declare.

Whoever will, may come to Him,
   Who died for all upon the tree,
And know His spirit to redeem,
   And His *free grace* to make them free!

Whoever shall in Him believe,
   And pard'ning mercy wait to prove,
Will surely life from Him receive,
   And know the riches of His love.

EXPECTATION.

"Even so, come Lord Jesus."

Rev. xxii. 20.

302. Come, Lord Jesus, quickly come,
   Haste to bring Thy people home;
Come, Thy righteous cause maintain,
   Thou whose right it is to reign.

Soon the world Thy rule shall see,
And shall worship only Thee;
It shall see Thy sceptre shine,
And the kingdom shall be Thine!

Bride and Spirit bid Thee come,
Haste, Thy kingly power assume;
Let the earth unite the strain,
Praise the Lamb who once was slain!

Come, " Desired of nations," come,
All Thy works the cry resume;
Let the world Thy glory see,
Serve and worship only Thee!

MISCELLANEOUS.

SUPPLICATION.

7's.

303. Holy Spirit, me inspire,
Fill me with celestial fire,
Write Thy truths upon my mind,
To my heart Thy precepts bind.

Graciously unto me show
All that Thou would'st have me know,
And prepare me to receive
All that Thou art wont to give.

Be my light and be my way,
Be my comfort and my stay,
Be my teacher and my friend,
Be my life that ne'er shall end.

Be my wisdom, guard, and guide,
Knowledge, faith, and pow'r beside;
All Thy grace to me be giv'n,
Felt on earth or known in heav'n.

PRAISE.

God's Omnipresence! Omniscience! and Omnipotence!

8's & 7's.

304. I will praise the Lord all-seeing,
　　He who doth my thoughts perceive,
　　He from whom I had my being,
　　And in whom alone I live.

I will praise the Lord all-knowing,
    Who knows all my works and ways,
Who, His gifts on me bestowing,
    A bounteous hand displays.

I will praise the Lord all-pow'rful,
    Whose creative pow'r and love,
Is unto all most wonderful,
    In the earth and heav'n above.

I will give Him thanks and blessing,
    By His grace my voice will raise,
And will praise Him without ceasing,
    Who is worthy of all praise.

THE TRIUNITY OF GOD.

Deut. vi. 4 ; 1 John v. 7.

305. Jehovah, the Almighty Lord,
    Who reigns on His eternal throne,
How great and powerful His Word,
    And Holy Spirit, which are One.

The God whom angels glorify,
    And mighty Cherubim adore,*
Who holy, holy, holy, cry,
    And worship Him for evermore.

A Trinity in Unity,
    The all-creating God is He ;
A Unity in Trinity,
    Now and to all eternity.

---

* In Hebrew "Cherub is singular ; Cherubim is plural."—A. CLARKE'S *Commentary on Eze.* x. 20.

"Cherubim the Hebrew plural of Cherub."—WALKER'S *Dictionary.*

WORSHIP AND ADORATION.
4-6's & 2-8's.

306. Unto the Lord above,
　　The Father with the Son,
And Spirit of His love,
　　The Holy Three in One,
Be praise and adoration given
By all on earth and all in heaven.

7's, 6's, 8's.

307. To Father, Word, and Spirit,
　　The great Almighty One,
Who made, and doth inherit,
　　And rule all worlds alone,
Worship by all to Him be paid,
As all from Him their being had!

L. M.

308. Praise the Almighty God above,
Praise Him in Christ, Son of His love:
The *triune* God as one adore,
And praise Him now and evermore.

L. M.

309. Now to the Father and the Son,
And Holy Spirit, Three in One,
Be highest praise and glory giv'n,
By all in earth and all in heav'n.

L. M.

310. Unto the Father, with the Son,
And Holy Spirit, ever One,
Be honor, praise, and glory giv'n
By all that dwell in earth and heav'n.

WORSHIP AND ADORATION.

7's.

311. Father, Son, and Holy Ghost,
　　In immortal union One,
　Worshipp'd by the heav'nly host,
　　On the everlasting throne;

　We also our praises bring,
　　We will worship and adore
　Thee the great eternal King,
　　Reigning now and evermore.

BENEDICTION.

7's, 6's, 8's.

312. O may the grace of Jesus,
　　And the great love of God,
　The Spirit's work within us,
　　Be felt and understood:
　The covenanted witnesses
　That His salvation we possess.

DIVINE LOVE.

L. M.

313. O love divine! what wondrous joy
　Does my enraptured thoughts employ,
　Is love so great in its increase
　That it will never, never cease?

　Yes, while eternity rolls on,
　The love of God, in Christ the Son,
　Like a vast ocean ever flows,
　And a decreasing never knows.

COMMEMORATION.
S. M.

314. With strains of joy I sing
　　The honors of my God,
The triumphs of my heav'nly King,
　　Wrought when He shed His blood.

While in the grave He lay,
　　How dismal was the sight,
Till He arose with pow'rful sway
　　And pierced the clouds of night.

Th' mighty Champion see
　　In royal strength array'd,
And joyful marks of victory
　　Are by His looks display'd.

The bloody fight is won,
　　And hell the terror feels,
Led captive by th' eternal Son,
　　Bound to His chariot wheels.

Hark to the trumpet's sound,*
　　Echoing as He flies,
While holy angels wait around
　　To shout Him to the skies!

There on His Father's throne
　　He sits with sov'reign power,
And looks till He shall reign alone
　　And foes be known no more!

PETITION.
C. M.

315. Lord give the understanding mind
　　And the receiving heart,
That Thy word may acceptance find
　　And savingly convert.

* Psa. xlvii. 5.

Shine with Thy light on minds obscure,
    The hardened souls reprove,
By all prevailing grace allure
    And bind with cords of love!

Then may Thy servants, Lord, be glad,
    And with rejoicings hail
A work which shall its' influence spread
    And mightily prevail.

Prevail as Thou shalt give it strength
    And fruit in ev'ry place,
Till all the tribes of men at length
    Together seek Thy face.

PETITION.

S. M.

316. Eternal *triune* Lord,
    Of power and grace and love,
Be Thou through all the earth ador'd
    As in the heav'ns above.

Bring Thy salvation nigh
    To all the earth-born race;
Pour out Thy spirit from on high
    And glorify Thy grace.

Now let Thy kingdom come
    To all that dwell below;
Thy universal Rule assume
    And make the nations bow.

Reign Thou o'er all the earth
    By Thy commanding rod,
From east to west, from south to north,
    As Thou alone art God!

May wars entirely cease
T" exalt Thy peaceful reign;
And perfect truth and righteousness
Thy sacred cause maintain.

May heav'n and earth as one
In Thy blest service move,
That all by whom Thy will is done
May know Thy reign of love!

PETITION.
C. M.

317. Almighty God, make bare Thine arm,
Thy day of power is come;
The word of prophecy confirm,
And bring Thy people home.

Where'er Thou hast the work begun,
Crown it with growing fame,
E'en from the rising of the sun
And setting of the same.

Send forth Thy messengers of grace
Girt with Thy Spirit's sword,
Till men of every name and place
Acknowledge Thee as Lord.

When all the earth Thy name shall know,
Thy power and glory see,
Joined in true unity below
And worship only Thee!

PRAISE AND PRAYER.
4-8's & 2-6's.

318. Mighty Creator hear our song,
It doth unto Thy Church belong,
To celebrate Thy praise.
We the chief objects of Thy care,
We who Thy richest bounties share,
For this our voices raise.

We gladly speak Thy praise, O Lord,
Who dost to us Thy help afford
　　In this delightful theme ;
Thou art our only trust and stay,
Our living hope, our heav'nly way,
　　And source of good supreme !

Oh, may we each give Thee our heart,
That we may ne'er from Thee depart,
　　Nor once provoke Thy rod ;
But in Thy fear and righteousness,
In faith and love and holiness,
　　Serve Thee the Lord our God.

Unite us to Thyself in love,
Our all-sufficient Saviour prove,
　　Till victory is given ;
Till all our foes are overcome,
And grace has brought us safely home
　　To rest and reign in heaven !

THE HARVEST SEASON.

8's.

319.　The Lord of the harvest appears
　　　　Reviving our beclouded hopes,
　　And allaying th' husbandman's fears,
　　　　As he stores the home-gathered crops.

The long visitation of rain
　　It has now passed over and gone,
The weather has cleared up again
　　And the sun in the heav'ns hath shone.

As our faith and patience were tried,
　　To murmur we knew would be wrong,
And that He who th' harvest supplied
　　Would not His correction prolong.

Our pray'rs in His mercy He heard,
　Which He hath in His goodness reveal'd,
As He to our uses hath spared
　The sustaining fruits of the field !

The sun from his chambers hath shone,
　And by his life-cheering bright rays
The tokens of sadness are gone,
　And a prospect of plenty displays.

Our gratitude then should be shown
　For th' needful supply of our wants,
And we by obedience own
　Th' unmerited favors He grants.

THE NEW YEAR.

6 lines 7's.

320. Lo ! another year has run
　　　Its appointed circuit round,
　　And the fast approaching sun
　　　Hastes to quit the narrow bound,
　　By his rising to display
　　Light upon the new year's day!

Ris'n his rapid course he steers,
　Pressing on without a stay,
While the months in their careers
　Moving onwards pass away ;
Swift in their unceasing flight,
Measures of the day and night.

As a tale our days we spend,
　And the seasons as they fly
Bring us nearer to our end,
　To our final destiny ;
Soon they land us on the shore
Where these changes are no more.

Let us then the time redeem,
  Catch the moments in their flight,
Always well improving them,
  Keeping still their end in sight:
That whene'er the time may come
Heav'n may be our endless home.

UNION THE CONSERVATOR OF PEACE.
C. M.

321. Unity is the bond of peace,
  Nor knows the sons of strife;
It is the all conserving grace,
  Of real inward life.

Let discord but an entrance gain
  To love's united band,
And peace will very soon be slain
  By her destroying hand.

The virgin of those sacred ties
  By which their souls are bound,
When forced to a desertion, flies
  Where cheering peace is found.

Contentions drive her far away
  To seek a resting place,
That she may there her sceptre sway,
  And show her smiling face.

SOLILOQUY.
L. M.

322. Arouse, my soul, thy energies,
  So may Thy quick'ned spirit live,
Seeking from Jesus, who supplies,
  And will restoring graces give.

What things are pure, what things are good,
    What things are needful for the soul,
By Christ alone must be bestow'd,
    Whose death hath merited the whole!

He is the source of heav'nly love,
    He is the spring of living power,
And in pure wisdom from above
    He doth His special graces shower.

Then look to Him with steadfast care,
    And trust His mercy ever sure,
To persevere in faith and prayer,
    And live to praise Him evermore.

THE RECLUSE, OR THE SEPARATION.
12 lines 8's.

323. Adieu, earth's vanities, adieu;
I may no longer such pursue;
Just observation will accrue,
And experience speaks it true,
In seeking such things here below,
But little else than troubles grow.
Wherefore in heart I leave that soil,
With all its vanity and toil,
Which oft the best laid efforts foil,
And make the sickened mind recoil,
Yea, make the careworn creature bow,
And sink the aspiring spirit low.

My mind no longer tarries here,
But lives where nobler treasures are,
And finds that better portion there,
Which puts an end to anxious care.
Here good I sought long time in vain,
I sought but never could obtain;
But now true happiness I find,
A solid good to fill the mind:

Knowledge with its attendants joined,
Honor and riches all combin'd,
With love and pleasure in the train,
True profit and eternal gain.

PRAYING FOR GRACE AND PRESERVATION.

6 lines 8's.

324. Great God of mercy and of love,
Who keepest covenant with those
That in Thy way Thy will approve,
And humble trust in Thee repose;
Preserve me by Thy power divine,
Lest I the path of life decline.

With trembling hesitating steps
I travel toward Thy holy hill,
And onward though my spirit keeps,
Faintness forebodes impending ill;
Oh, grant me Thy sustaining grace,
And quicken me t' amend my pace.

Direct my feet with cheerful speed
Toward the kingdom of Thy joy,
And let me, from this darkness freed,
My light'ned pow'rs for Thee employ :
Acceptably Thy praises show,
And glorify Thy name below.

Lord grant to me this one request,
That I, by grace being prepar'd,
May enter Thy eternal rest
And share the infinite reward :
With all that shall participate
The glory of the heav'nly state.

PRAYING FOR PRESERVATION.
6 lines S's.

325. Help us, O Lord, to watch and pray,
To work while it is called to day,
Lest unexpected darkness come
To make us stumble in the way
And lead our erring steps astray,
So hinder us from reaching home.

Oh, help us all to persevere,
With courage firm and hearts sincere,
Until we meet before Thy face;
Where we shall reign in glory bright,
Absorbed in pleasures of delight!
And visions of eternal peace!

SPIRITUAL MEDITATIONS.
L. M.

326. New scenes of wonder and of joy,
My grateful heart and tongue employ;
Since Jesus and redeeming love
My constant theme and portion prove.

His candle shining on my head,
Illuminates the path I tread;
His sacred finger points my way,
And leads me on to brighter day

Increasing pleasures do I know,
Increasing happiness below,
While cloudless joys remain above,
The happy world to which I move.

New scenes unto my view disclose,
Sweet scenes of glory and repose;
Nor will eternity be found
Too long the depths of love to sound!

THE ENCHANTRESS!

"The pleasures of sin." Heb.
And "the deceitfulness of sin."

C. M.

327. She has a thousand treach'rous charms
   To her deluded throng,
Enticing with her fondling arms,
   And her bewitching tongue.

Happy she sings is ev'ry man,
   And ev'ry woman too,
That will approve my secret plan
   And all my favors woo.

Let not your lives be buried in
   The gloom of anxious care,
When you can taste the sweets of sin
   And find such pleasures there.

They list to her enchanting song,
   Which, acting as a spell,
Her victims they are lured along
   The downward road to hell.

Hear now, ye captive souls, and take
   This warning from my lips,
And all your loving sins forsake,
   For there your mis'ry sleeps.

Her smiles and her caresses now
   Of such a tempting air,
May soon to grief and sorrow grow
   And end in black despair.

For sin is a deceitful foe,
   And a beguiling friend,
Its fruits will turn to gall and woe,
   Most bitter in the end.

WARNING.

C. M.

328. How little doth the sinner think,
On evil pleasures bent,
He sports on ruin's awful brink
With endless punishment.

With a dark mind and conscience sear'd,
He treads the downward path,
As if he impiously dar'd
T" defy his Maker's wrath;

Regardless of those inward stings,
Which leave a ling'ring smart,
He still pursues forbidden things
And hardens his own heart!

Yet these, his wayward actions will,
Create an aching void,
Which nothing that he seeks can fill
Though seemingly enjoyed.

We warn him of the hidden woes
Which now his steps attend,
And that his friends will prove his foes
Is certain in the end.

Let him reflect and turn his feet
Into the way of peace,
For there he will free mercy meet,
And find true happiness.

INVITATION.

329. Come, ye weary souls and wretched,
Leave your doubts and fears behind,
Lo! the Saviour's arms are stretch'd,
He is pitiful and kind,
See in Jesus you may all compassion find!

Do you deem yourselves unworthy
   Of His mercy, as you say,
You will then receive it freely,
   And there is no other way!
     Oh, believe it, doubt it not, nor make delay!

Do you feel your inward blindness?
   Fear you cannot come to Him?
Farther still extends His kindness,
   Though but weak your faith may seem:
     He will help you who hath promis'd to redeem.

He will quick remove the mountain
   Separating you from God,
And disclose the living fountain
   Flowing with His precious blood:
     Wash and cleanse you in the all-availing flood.

By His Word He doth invite you,
   Cries, "Poor sinners come to me;"
And His Spirit doth entreat you
   To partake His mercy free;
     Peace and pardon ev'ry grace in Jesus see!

Oh! renounce your hesitation,
   Leave your feelings of dismay,
Now accept His great salvation
   In His own appointed way:
     And you will rejoice and bless the happy day.

ENCOURAGEMENT.

S. M.

330. Ho! ye despairing ones,
     On whom compassion leans,
    Behold the Saviour's blood atones
     For your much dreaded sins.

Jesus, in mighty love,
  Will grant you a release,
He will your guilty fears remove
  And make your torments cease.

From sorrow's weeping eye,
  From all desponding care,
From sinful crimes of deepest dye,
  His mercy deigns to spare!

His Spirit will reveal
  And inward light impart,
The pearl of His forgiveness seal
  On each believing heart.

No longer then refrain
  To come before His face,
But trace through your Redeemer's pain
  His reconciling grace.

His favor will be giv'n
  With peace and quietness,
And everlasting life in heav'n,
  In truth and faithfulness.

THE SOLEMNITY OF DEATH.

C. M.

331. The tolling knell with chilling sound
  Salutes my list'ning ear,
And its solemnity profound
  Excites an humble fear.

It tells me I am born to die,
  That in a little space,
I with the sleeping dead must lie
  And end this mortal race.

But the time when, or where, or how,
  Is hidden and concealed,
And loudly calls upon me now
  To walk by *light* revealed!

Obedience unto God will sure,
  Through faith in Jesus' love,
A mansion in th' heavens secure,
  Which never can remove.

THE DYING CHRISTIAN.

S. M.

332. And is the time arrived,
  The happy period come,
That I must die, and be received
  To an unfading home?

Angels are waiting now
  My Spirit to remove,
From scenes of sorrow here below,
  To realms of joy above.

I triumph in the Lord,
  Who victory hath giv'n,
And resting on His saving Word,*
  Depart in peace to heav'n.

A VOICE FROM THE GRAVE.

6's.

333. Time was, when I beheld
  These mansions of the dead,
But now my eyes are seal'd,
  And life from me has fled.

* Jas. i. 21; 1 Pet. i. 23—25.

My dust, which lies below,
    In such a narrow space,
Will to the living show
    Their future lot and place.

Oh, you that read these lines,
    Seek while the hour is giv'n,
Ere light and life declines,
    To make your peace with heav'n.

In Jesus Christ believe,
    Who died your souls to save,
To Him your service give,
    And live beyond the grave!

FAREWELL.*

7's.

F arewell now my readers all,
A nd I pray you understand,
R uminating on the call
E ach one has to Canaan's land:
W hile the end you ponder well,
E ach some truths the other tell,
L earning as you travel home
L essons of the world to come!

FINIS.

F avored are the sons of God,
I n inheriting by grace,
N eedful, and all promised, good
I n the end of this their race,
S ettled and secured by grace.

* 2 Cor. xiii. 11.

INDEX.

GENESIS NO.
   In the beginning God hath said 1
   God created the sun and moon 2
   God, He created ev'ry beast 3
   Man in God's image made 4
   Awake, my soul, and sound His praise 5
   When Adam in Paradise stood 6
   While in Eden our parents remained 7
   When Abel offer'd sacrifice 8
   Enoch most truly served the Lord 9
   When the old world was lost and drown'd . . . 10
   He who the universe sustains 11
   By th' beautiful bow in the cloud 12
   Nimrod, the Ruler, fam'd of old 13
   Abraham left his father's home 14
   My great and exceeding reward 15
   When Sodom and Gomorrah sinn'd 16
   Abraham went at God's command 17
   Abraham was the friend of God 18

EXODUS
   What mighty wonders have been done 19
   The sacred paschal lamb 20
   When Moses smote the rock of old 21
   Moses, the rock in Horeb smote 22
   Amalek, the foe of Israel 23
   When Amalek went out and fought 24
   Jehovah on Mount Sinai spake 25

NUMBERS
   When at their sacred feast the Jews 26
   Spring up, O earthly well 27
   This well was a type of God's well 28

DEUTERONOMY
   Hark, my soul, thy Saviour speaks 29
   The table of the Lord 30
   The God of the heavens is nigh 31

JOSHUA
	No.
Old Jericho, once walled around	32
Jericho, rebuilt where it stood	33
Who will deny that th' sun stood still	34

2 SAMUEL
The man who had a well	35
The far-fam'd well of Bethlehem	36

1 KINGS
Jehovah, He is God	37
Elijah, by ravens was fed	38

2 KINGS
Elijah taken up to heaven	39
To heaven, Elijah was borne.	40
Th' chariot of Israel is love	41
Samaria of old, besieged	42

1 CHRONICLES
Jabez, a child of sorrow born	43
Jabez, a humble child	44
David, like other warriors, had	45
The noted well of Beth-lehem	46

JOB
Upright was holy Job	47
Mankind unto trouble are born	48
Our time is ever on the wing	49
Man who is of a woman born	50
Thou king of all terrors to man	51
I know that my Redeemer lives	52
Oh that it were with me	53
If God himself our teacher is	54

PSALMS
The fool, who in his heart hath said	55
In the presence of God	56
The firmament on high	57
Great are the works of God	58
O Thou that hear'st the sinner's prayer	59
Press'd with sin and sorrow's weight	60
I'll praise the Lord always	61
The righteous many trials have	62
The Lord is my deliverer	63
Why art thou cast down, my soul	64
My heart good matter will indite	65
My heart a good theme shall indite	66

PSALMS—*continued.* NO.

Awake, my soul, a grateful lay 67
Let God in strength arise 68
How solemn is the thought 69
Alas, our mortal state 70
Father, how kind Thy dealings are 71
O bless the Lord, my soul 72
Death hurries all its sons to dust 73
Praise ye the heav'nly King 74
How shall a young man cleanse his way? . . . 75
Quicken my soul, O Lord 76
Lord, how I love Thy law 77
Great peace have they that love Thy law . . . 78
Except the Lord shall build the house . . . 79
The Monarch that rules in heav'n 80
God is great and of great power 81

PROVERBS

Drink thine own waters flowing 82
Hark, from the regions of the skies . . . 83
If the cry of the poor is not heard 84
Pardon, O Lord, the crimes 85

ECCLESIASTES

In the beautiful blossoming earth 86
Death soon removes us out of time 87
May th' voice of the preacher be heard . . . 88
We hear the preacher say 89
Rejoice, O young man, in thy youth 90

CANTICLES

Sweet as the rose of Sharon's fields 91
Thy name, as ointment, is pour'd forth . . . 92

ISAIAH

House of the Lord, exalted high 93
Cease my soul to look to man 94
Come tune a lofty strain 95
The Lord on high proclaims 96
Alpha and Omega, He 97
Christ is the great Prince of Peace 98
God's people will Him praise 99
We living waters draw with joy 100
Ye messengers of the most High 101
O Babylon, thy mighty name 102
When God His ensign lifteth up 103
On the mountain of God 104
When the great trumpet shall be blown . . . 105

ISAIAH—*continued.*   NO.

See the Church built on the rock 106
As parent birds protect their young 107
Behold the ensign of the Lord 108
Behold the ensign of the Lord 109
How beautiful and glorious 110
The watchmen shall lift up their voice 111
Jesus, with glory crowned 112
Mount Zion may be desolate 113
Ho, ev'ry one that thirsteth come 114
Is this th' fast that I have chosen? 115
The holy city of our God 116
Darkness covereth the earth 117
Who is this from Edom comes 118
Just as the leaf fadeth away 119

JEREMIAH

Hark, from on high the trumpet sounds 120
Is there no balm in Gilead? 121
The true balm of Gilead is grace 122
Jehovah He alone is God 123
Vile and deceitful is man's heart 124
God's Word's a living fire 125
Just like a hammer He 126

EZEKIEL

Come from the winds, reviving breath 127

DANIEL

Behold the *image* of the Kings 128
The lion beast with eagle's wings 129
Behold ten horns upon the beast 130
See ten horns, which mean ten kings 131
Behold the little horn 132
Lord of the worlds of light 133

HOSEA

How shall I give thee up, saith God? 134

MICAH

Arise ye and depart 135
The breaker, He is come 136
The breaker by His might 137
The breaker manifested hath 138
He breaks the great red Dragon's power . . . 139
When from their hills and mountains too . . . 140
God unto men hath shown 141
God by His *light* hath plainly show'd 142

JONAH
    NO.
    Jonah, a prophet sent by the Lord 143

NAHUM
    The lion gloating o'er his prey 144

HABAKKUK
    Revive Thy work, O Lord 145

ZEPHANIAH
    Since the confounding of men's tongues. . . . 146

ZECHARIAH
    The stone, very precious and bright 147
    Turn you to the strong hold 148
    Against my fellow, saith the Lord 149
    Rejoice ye righteous in the Lord 150

MALACHI
    Let Britons sound aloud 151
    Not one thing hath fail'd to me 152

MATTHEW
    Let notes of honor swell 153
    Blessed are the peacemakers 154
    The yearly feast, the Passover 155
    Give to him that asketh thee 156
    Prayer is not discovered in words 157
    God of mercy and salvation 158
    How many thousands walk the road 159
    The tree by its fruit is declar'd 160
    Not ev'ry one that saith Lord, Lord 161
    Lord of the winds and waves 162
    Weary sinners go to God 163
    Behold th' meek and lowly Saviour 164
    Hosanna to King David's Son 165
    Iniquity triumphs and reigns 166
    Hark the Judgment trumpet speaks 167
    When at the yearly Jewish feast 168
    Christians who think they stand secure . . . 169
    Jesus, who suffered death for men 170
    Behold the Christ, the Holy One 171

MARK
    Be not afraid, ye doubting souls 172
    Alas, my soul, what horror reigns 173
    Pray we all unto the Lord 174

LUKE

	NO.
Jesus was of a virgin born	175
Emmanuel appear'd	176
Physician of the sin-sick soul	177
The foxes have holes for their home	178
Th' man that from Jerusalem went	179
While Mary sat to hear her Lord	180
Pour out Thy spirit, Lord	181
The gate of life to enter	182
Behold the prodigal	183
Now let the fatted calf be slain	184
See Lazarus the beggar laid	185
The Pharisee devoutly prayed	186
The Publican, with grief and shame	187
As Jesus passed near Jericho	188
The signs of Jesus' coming	189

JOHN

Beside the pool of gospel love	190
Before Bethesda's pool	191
Jesus, risen from the dead	192
As Jesus is the living bread	193
In heart alone can we believe	194
What said He, who was the first	195
Unto our prayers attend	196
What is truth? one asked of old	197

ACTS

The name of the Lord is His pow'r	198
Shine from Thy sacred seat, O Lord	199
Guilty, helpless, and distressed	200
The Lord the commandment hath giv'n	201
The message of our God	202

ROMANS

The Gospel is the power of God	203
He is the true and living Jew	204
How frail we mortals are	205

1 CORINTHIANS

Not mortal eye hath seen	206
Christ, our passover, is slain	207
Now while the sun shines clear and bright	208
Jesus is the living Rock	209
Thou watcher of my soul	210
And must this body die	211
God's spirit shows a mystery	212

		NO.
2 CORINTHIANS		
Many are the promises		213
EPHESIANS		
Jesus of His Church is Head		214
It is through faith that we are saved		215
God He foresaw the fall of man		216
Almighty God of love		217
Be circumspect in your talk		218
PHILIPPIANS		
Come, my Saviour, quickly come		219
Let th' servants of Jesus rejoice		220
2 THESSALONIANS		
Him who after Satan cometh		221
1 TIMOTHY		
Th' Bible speaks of a mediator		222
Religion makes our happiness		223
HEBREWS		
Lord, what is man whom Thou hast made		224
Now in the day of Christ the Lord		225
To-day if ye will hear		226
The Sabbath was a type		227
The Sabbath is God's day of rest		228
When th' Tabernacle was erected		229
While the Tabernacle stood		230
Patience is needful to the saints		231
When Abel his first off'ring made		232
JAMES		
How swift and hasty is our life		233
Faith without works is dead		234
How full of evil is the tongue		235
1 PETER		
He is ris'n again from the dead		236
Poor souls, in their dark prison-house		237
2 PETER		
No tongue can speak nor words can tell		238
1 JOHN		
With hatred harbored in the breast		239
Fountain of bliss, unmeasured love		240
Blest be the fountain of Thy love		241
My soul mounts up on eagle's wings		242
True Christians know one God		243
Men have hearts quite full of evil		244
How full of darkness, sin and woe		245

REVELATION

	NO.
Behold the seven lamps of fire	246
He who hath the key of David	247
Jehovah in majesty reigns	248
Great God, with trembling awe I bow	249
Now to the King whose power supreme	250
The Lamb He openeth the seals	251
The Lamb who hath seven horns	252
Behold the Lamb who hath sev'n horns	253
When Angels join to praise the Lord	254
Worthy is the Lamb that was slain	255
When the seventh seal is broken	256
Behold a mountain burning	257
A mighty Angel cometh down	258
The living witnesses for God	259
Attend the seventh trumpet's sound	260
Hark, the seventh trumpet sounds	261
Behold a wonder seen in heav'n	262
Seven heads the Dragon has	263
Who cometh from the wilderness	264
See the monster Beast uprising	265
Behold the beast that's like a Lamb	266
He who cometh like a Lamb	267
Lo! "Here is wisdom" saith the Lord	268
Now the gospel word is giv'n	269
Listen to the voice of God	270
A voice which spake from heav'n is heard	271
How glorious th' prospect of saints at their death	272
How happy are the saints	273
Sweet is th' memory of the dead	274
An angel sits on a *white* cloud	275
Great and marvellous are Thy acts	276
Arise, my soul, with all thy pow'rs	277
Now we arise, and sing the song	278
The first vial when pour'd forth	279
The vial pour'd in judgment forth	280
Lo! the seventh angel pours	281
Mystery, Babylon the great	282
A mighty Angel now descends	283
Great Babylon shall fall	284
All heav'n and earth their voices raise	285
Loud Hallelujah's now we sing	286
His name is call'd the Word of God	287
His name is call'd the Word of God	288
From the high throne of God in heav'n	289
A song of triumph now is heard	290
Glory in the Lord your God	291
The King of kings and Lord of lords	292

REVELATION—*continued.*

	NO.
When John, who in a heav'nly vision	293
He who wears many crowns on high	294
An angel standing in the sun	295
An angel standing in the sun	296
Hark! a voice the trumpet soundeth	297
Zion, the city of our God	298
In the glad City of the Lord	299
Blessed are those that do obey	300
The Spirit and the Bride say Come	301
Come, Lord Jesus, quickly come	302

MISCELLANEOUS

Holy Spirit, me inspire	303
I will praise the Lord all-seeing	304
Jehovah, the Almighty Lord	305
Unto the Lord above	306
To Father, Word, and Spirit	307
Praise the Almighty God above	308
Now to the Father and the Son	309
Unto the Father, with the Son	310
Father, Son, and Holy Ghost	311
O may the grace of Jesus	312
O love divine! what wondrous joy	313
With strains of joy I sing	314
Lord give the understanding mind	315
Eternal *triune* Lord	316
Almighty God, make bare Thine arm	317
Mighty Creator hear our song	318
The Lord of the harvest appears	319
Lo! another year has run	320
Unity is the bond of peace	321
Arouse, my soul, thy energies	322
Adieu, earth's vanities, adieu	323
Great God of mercy and of love	324
Help us, O Lord, to watch and pray	325
New scenes of wonder and of joy	326
She has a thousand treach'rous charms	327
How little doth the sinner think	328
Come, ye weary souls and wretched	329
Ho! ye despairing ones	330
The tolling knell with chilling sound	331
And is the time arrived	332
Time was, when I beheld	333

www.ingramcontent.com/pod-product-compliance
Lightning Source LLC
Chambersburg PA
CBHW031933230426
43672CB00010B/1910